Handbook of Ceremonies

Dag Heward-Mills

Parchment House

HANDBOOK OF CEREMONIES

First published 2017 by Parchment House
2nd Printing 2018

Find out more about Dag Heward-Mills at:

Healing Jesus Campaign
Email: evangelist@daghewardmills.org
Website: www.daghewardmills.org
Facebook: Dag Heward-Mills
Twitter: @EvangelistDag

ISBN : 978-9988-8503-2-6

Contents

CHAPTER 1

Naming Ceremony

The Naming Ceremony is a traditional event that takes place after the birth of a child. Some families are very traditional and abide by all customs relating to the date and time of the event. The pastor's role is basically to introduce a biblical and spiritual perspective to the occasion. This of course is only possible depending on what the family requests or allows.

1. OPENING PRAYER

2. WORSHIP : Come Let Us Adore Him

O come let us adore Him	*For He alone is worthy*
O come let us adore Him	*For He alone is worthy*
O come let us adore Him	*For He alone is worthy*
Christ the Lord	*Christ the Lord*

By John Francis Wade

3. REASON FOR OCCASION

We are gathered here today with our brother and sister, Mr. and Mrs. ...(Last name of parents)... for two reasons:

i. To rejoice over what God has done for them and

ii. To give a name to their newly born baby.

The Bible is the basis for whatever we do, therefore, our scripture reading for today is:

Luke 1:57-64

Now Elisabeth's full time came that she should be delivered; and she brought forth a son. And her neighbours and her cousins heard how the Lord had shewed great mercy upon her; and they rejoiced with her.

And it came to pass, that on the eighth day they came to circumcise the child; and they called him Zacharias, after the name of his father. And his mother answered and said, Not so; but he shall be called John. And they said unto her, There is none of thy kindred that is called by this name. And they made signs to his father, how he would have him called. And he asked for a writing table, and wrote, saying, His name is John. And they marvelled all. And his mouth was opened immediately, and his tongue loosed, and he spake, and praised God.

As was done in those days, we want to call on the father of the child to give us the name(s) he desires to give to the child and the meaning(s) of the name(s).

4.   GIVING   OF NAME BY FATHER [Father stands up and mentions the full name of the child and the meaning(s) of the name(s)].

5.   PROCLAMATION,   SANCTIFICATION   AND AFFIRMATION OF NAME ON THE CHILD

i. Minister takes the baby and asks all to stand and join in prayer for the baby.

ii. Minister prays laying hands on the baby, and anoints the baby with oil.

6.   PRAYER

MINISTER: Father, in the name of Jesus, thine only begotten Son, we thank you for the name(s) that has been given today. We sanctify this name(s) and we declare that this child shall be called ...[name(s) of child].... From today I pray that he shall live up to the meaning(s) of this name(s).

The Minister makes reference to the name(s) and prays for the child to fulfil the purpose of the name. (e.g., "John means 'Jehovah is gracious', May Jehovah God be gracious unto this child always.")

MINISTER: I anoint this baby with oil as a symbol of the Holy Spirit, that he may live under the influence and power of the Holy Spirit, all the days of his life. Amen.

7.   SONG: Showers of Blessing

	Chorus
There shall be showers of blessing;	*Showers of blessing*
This is the promise of God	*Showers of blessing we plead*
There shall be seasons refreshing,	*Mercy drops round us are falling*
Sent from the Saviour above	*But for the showers we plead*
	By Daniel W. Whittle

3

8. BLESSING OF THE CHILD

MINISTER: Father, we thank you indeed for a good and perfect gift, the gift of a life. Thank you for blessing this family with this child. I cancel, I nullify, I reverse, and I reject every curse and every expectation of the enemy concerning the life of ...[name(s) of child]....

I bring down the walls of opposition, resistance, and frustration that are lifted up against the life of this child. I superimpose the will of God over and against every plan, every projection and prediction of the enemy for your life.

I speak the blessing of God over your life.

May the goodness and the favour of God be your portion all the days of your life.

May you live to be a blessing to your parents.

May you live to be a blessing to your generation.

May you become what God has destined you to be. In Jesus' mighty name. Amen.

9. CHARGE TO PARENTS

MINISTER: Do you promise to bring up this child in the ways of the Lord that he may not depart from them when he grows?

According to Deuteronomy 6:7, do you promise to "teach him the Word of God when thou sittest in thine house, and when thou walkest by the way, and when thou liest down, and when thou risest up?"

FATHER: I do.

MOTHER: I do.

BOTH PARENTS TOGETHER: We do.

MINISTER: Amen! Shall we clap for them? (Minister returns the baby to the parents.)

10.   SONG: To God be the Glory

To God be the glory,
Great things He hath done
So loved He the world that
He gave us His Son
Who yielded His life
* an atonement for sin*
And opened the life gate
that all may go in

Chorus
Praise the Lord! Praise the Lord!
Let the earth hear His voice
Praise the Lord! Praise the Lord!
Let the People rejoice
O come to the Father through Jesus the
Son
And give Him the glory great things
He hath done

Lyrics by Fanny Crossby (1875)

11.   PRESENTATION OF GIFTS

MINISTER: Now, as it was done when Jesus was born, wise men came from the east with precious gifts.

We shall now receive the gifts and presents that have been brought for the child.

12.   CLOSING PRAYER

CHAPTER 2

Baby Dedication Ceremony

The dedication of babies is similar to the Naming Ceremony. This is usually conducted during a service in church.

The dedication takes place after the birth of the child. The minister's role in the Baby Dedication is to pray over the child and dedicate it to the Lord. This is done with the hope that when the child is of age he himself will come to know the Lord Jesus Christ.

The Minister commits the child into the Lord's care and presents the names and their meanings to the congregation.

1. **WELCOME THE FAMILY TO THE ALTAR** (Officiating Minister introduces the family to the congregation).

2. **REASON FOR OCCASION**

MINISTER: We are gathered here today with our brother and sister, Mr. and Mrs. ...(Last name of parents)... for three reasons:

   i.   Rejoice over what God has done for them,

   ii. To give a name to their newly born baby and

   iii. To dedicate this child unto the Lord.

MINISTER: As the Bible teaches, we will call on the father of the child to give us the name(s) of the child and the meaning(s) of the name(s).

3. **ASK FATHER FOR THE NAME** [Father mentions the full name of the child and the meaning(s) of the name(s).]

4. **PROCLAMATION, SANCTIFICATION AND AFFIRMATION OF NAME ON THE CHILD**

   • Minister takes the baby and asks all to join in prayer for the baby.

   • Minister lays his hand on the child and prays.

5. **PRAYER**

MINISTER: Father, in the name of Jesus, thine only begotten Son, we thank you for the name(s) that has been given today. We sanctify this name and we declare that this child shall be called [name(s) of child] From today I pray that he shall live up to the meaning of this name(s).

(The Minister makes reference to the name(s) and prays for the child to fulfil the purpose of the name(s), e.g., "John means 'Jehovah is gracious', May Jehovah God be gracious unto this child always.")

6.   PRAYER BLESSING OF CHILD

MINISTER: Father, we thank you indeed for a good and perfect gift; the gift of a life. Thank you for blessing this family with this child. I reject every curse and every expectation of the enemy concerning the life of [name(s) of child].

I bring down the walls of frustration that are lifted up against the life of this child. I superimpose the will of God for this child, over and against every plan of Satan.

I speak the blessing of God over this life. May the goodness and the favour of God be your portion all the days of your life.

May you live to be a blessing to your parents.

May you live to be a blessing to your generation.

May you become what God has destined you to be.

In Jesus' mighty name.

Amen.

CHAPTER 3

Water Baptism

Water Baptism is an important spiritual landmark in every Christian's life. It is one of the few ordinances that Christians are expected to perform. The pastor is expected to ensure that all Christians under his care have been duly baptized. It is also important to have a good understanding of the biblical and spiritual significance of this event. Water Baptism can be performed by those designated to do so.

INSTRUCTIONS FOR CANDIDATES:

1. Both men and ladies are not to wear only underwear.

2. No swimming costumes should be allowed.

3. No bare-chested men or ladies should be allowed.

4. All ladies must be fully covered.

INSTRUCTIONS FOR BAPTIZER:

1.   The baptiser should not be bare-chested or in underwear but must be fully and properly dressed.

INSTRUCTIONS ON IMMERSION:

1.   Tell the candidate to hold nose and close eyes.

2.   Baptiser holds candidate with one hand behind candidate, and the other hand on the forehead. Baptiser fully immerses candidate in water and raises him up again.

1.   OPENING PRAYER

2.   REASONS FOR BAPTISM

MINISTER: We are gathered here today to baptize these believers according to the Word of God. The basis for baptism is:

i. To obey the Word of God.

ii. It is one of the requirements after being Born Again. (Acts 8:36-38).

iii. It is an outward sign of what has happened to you spiritually. (Colossians 2:12).

iv. To fulfil all righteousness.

SCRIPTURES:

(i) Mark 16:16

He that believeth and is baptized shall be saved; but he that believeth not shall be damned.

(ii) Acts 10:47,48

Can any man forbid water, that these should not be baptized, which have received the Holy Ghost as well as we? And he commanded them to be baptized in the name of the Lord...

(iii) Acts 8: 36-38

And as they went on their way, they came unto a certain water: and the eunuch said, See, here is water; what doth hinder me to be baptized? And Philip said, If thou believest with all thine heart, thou mayest. And he answered and said, I believe that Jesus Christ is the Son of God ...and they went down both into the water, both Philip and the eunuch; and he baptized him.

(iv) Colossians 2:12

Buried with him in baptism, wherein also ye are risen with him through the faith of the operation of God, who hath raised him from the dead.

(v) Matthew 3:15-16

...Suffer it to be so now: for thus it becometh us to fulfil all righteousness. Then he suffered him. And Jesus, when he was baptized, went up straightway out of the water: and, lo, the heavens were opened unto him, and he saw the Spirit of God descending...

3. ASK THE BAPTISMAL CANDIDATE THE FOLLOWING QUESTIONS:

i.   Are you Born Again?

ii. Have you received Christ as your personal Saviour?

iii. Do you believe that Jesus died for you on the cross and that He rose again?

iv. Do you believe that Jesus Christ will be coming again to take His church away?

If you get a negative answer to any of the following questions:

- Abort the Baptismal ceremony immediately

- Lead the individual to accept Christ as his Saviour

- You may continue to baptize the individual if he genuinely receives the Lord as Saviour)

4. **ENTER THE WATER WITH THE BAPTISMAL CANDIDATE**

5. **LEAD THE BAPTISMAL CANDIDATE IN THE FOLLOWING CONFESSION:**

- I am a Born Again Christian. I believe that Jesus died for me and that He rose from the dead on the third day.

- By faith, I believe that all my sins are washed away in the blood of Jesus.

- I believe that my name is in the Book of Life.

- I am now looking for and expecting the return of my Master and Saviour, Jesus Christ, who will come in the clouds to take away His own.

- As I go down into the water I identify myself with the death and burial of Jesus Christ. As I come up out of the water I identify myself with the resurrection of the Lord.

- I am being baptized to fulfil all righteousness as the Lord Himself did.

6. **IMMERSE THE BAPTISMAL CANDIDATE FULLY IN THE WATER** (Ensure that he is fully submerged. Ask him to hold his breath and his nose as he is immersed.)

7. **PRAYER AFTER CANDIDATE HAS CHANGED**

8. **BRIEF TIME OF WORSHIP AND THANKSGIVING**

9. **CLOSING PRAYER**

CHAPTER 4

Communion Service

The cup of blessing which we bless, is it not the communion of the blood of Christ? The bread which we break, is it not the communion of the body of Christ?

1 Corinthians 10:16

EIGHT-POINT FORMAT FOR COMMUNION

1. PRAYER

2. PURPOSE

(i) 1 Corinthians 11:23-29

For I have received of the Lord that which also I delivered unto you, That the Lord Jesus the same night in which he was betrayed took bread: And when he had given thanks, he brake it, and said, Take, eat: this is my body, which is broken for you: this do in remembrance of me.

After the same manner also he took the cup, when he had supped, saying, This cup is the new testament in my blood: this do ye, as oft as ye drink it, in remembrance of me.

For as often as ye eat this bread, and drink this cup, ye do shew the Lord's death till he come. Wherefore whosoever shall eat this bread, and drink this cup of the Lord, unworthily, shall be guilty of the body and blood of the Lord. But let a man examine himself, and so let him eat of that bread, and drink of that cup. For he that eateth and drinketh unworthily, eateth and drinketh damnation to himself, not discerning the Lord's body.

(ii) John 6:51-56

I am the living bread which came down from heaven: if any man eat of this bread, he shall live for ever: and the bread that I will give is my flesh, which I will give for the life of the world. The Jews therefore strove among themselves, saying, How can this man give us his flesh to eat?

Then Jesus said unto them, Verily, verily, I say unto you, Except ye eat the flesh of the Son of man, and drink his blood, ye have no life in you. Whoso eateth my flesh, and drinketh my blood, hath eternal life; and I will raise him up at the last day.

For my flesh is meat indeed, and my blood is drink indeed.
He that eateth my flesh, and drinketh my blood, dwelleth
in me, and I in him.

3.   SONG: Sons of God

Chorus

Brothers, sisters we are one	*Sons of God, hear His Holy Word*
And our life has just begun	*Gather round the table of the Lord*
In the Spirit we are one	*Eat his body, drink his blood*
We can live forever	*And we'll sing a song of love*
	Hallu, hallelu, hallelu, hallelujah!

Chorus

Shout together to the Lord	*Sons of God, hear His Holy Word*
He has promised our reward	*Gather round the table of the Lord*
Happiness a hundred fold	*Eat his body, drink his blood*
And we'll live forever	*And we'll sing a song of love*
	Hallu, hallelu, hallelu, hallelujah!

By James Thiem

4.   KNEELING AND PRAYER OVER BREAD AND WINE : SHARING OF BREAD AND WINE TO ALL

5.   LIFTING AND EATING OF BREAD

(i) Luke 22:19

And Jesus took bread, and gave thanks, and brake it, and gave unto them, saying, this is my body which is given for you: this do in remembrance of me.

6.   LIFTING AND DRINKING OF WINE

(ii) Matthew 26:27-28

And He took the cup, and gave thanks, and gave it to them, saying, Drink ye all of it; For this is My blood of the new testament, which is shed for many for the remission of sins.

7.   PRAYER

8. SONG: The Old Rugged Cross

Chorus

On a hill far away,
Stood an old rugged cross
The emblem of suffering and shame
And I love that old rugged cross
Where the dearest and best
For a world of lost sinners was slain

So I'll cherish the old rugged cross;
Till my tophies at last I lay down
I will cling to the old rugged cross
And exchange it someday for a crown

By George Bennard

CHAPTER 5

Dedication of Homes, Businesses, Shops, etc.

At varying times in the ministry, members will ask the minister to impart God's blessing on their new homes, businesses or shops.

The pastor's role is to bless, sanctify and dedicate the business or home into the Lord's hand. This dedication takes place on the actual site and is marked by the pouring of oil on the site as a symbol of the Holy Spirit's blessing.

1.   OPENING PRAYER

2.   SONG: To God Be the Glory

To God be the glory,	**Chorus:**
Great things He hath done	*Praise the Lord! Praise the Lord!*
So loved He the world that	*Let the earth hear His voice*
He gave us His Son	*Praise the Lord! Praise the Lord,*
Who yielded His life	*Let the people rejoice*
An atonement for sin	*O come to the Father*
And opened the life gate	*through Jesus the Son*
that all may go in	*And give Him the glory great things*
	He hath done

By Fanny Crossby

3.   PURPOSE

i.   We acknowledge that the work has ended by God's grace.

1 Kings 7:51

So was ended all the work that king Solomon made for the house of the LORD. And Solomon brought in the things which David his father had dedicated...

ii. We acknowledge the ministers or elders of the church who are assembled together to pray and dedicate the project.

1 Kings 8:1,3

Then Solomon assembled the elders of Israel and all the heads of the tribes, the chief of the fathers of the children of Israel... all the elders of Israel came, and the priests took up the ark.

iii. We acknowledge God's faithfulness in completing the project.

1 Kings 8:1,22-24

And Solomon stood... in the presence of all the congregation of Israel, and spread forth his hands toward heaven: and he said LORD God of Israel, there is no God like thee...

who keepest covenant and mercy with thy servants that walk before thee with all their heart... thou speakest also with thy mouth, and hast fulfiled it with thine hand, as it is this day.

iv. We dedicate the project to the Lord, asking for God's presence to continually remain there.

2 Chronicles 6:40-42

Now, my God ... arise, O LORD God, into thy resting place... O LORD God, turn not away the face of thine anointed...

v. We ask for God's continued blessing in every undertaking.

1 Kings 8:35-36

When heaven is shut up, and there is no rain... if they pray ... and confess thy name... Then hear thou in heaven, and forgive the sin of thy servants... that thou teach them the good way wherein they should walk...

vi. We anoint the premises with oil and declare God's blessings on the project.

4.   INVITE HOME/BUSINESS OWNER TO GIVE INTRODUCTORY REMARKS

i. The reason for the occasion.

ii. A testimony of God's provision.

5.   SCRIPTURE READING

Deuteronomy 8:2,7-18

And thou shalt remember all the way which the LORD thy God led thee these forty years in the wilderness,to humble thee, and to prove thee, to know what was in thine heart, whether thou wouldest keep his commandments, or no. For the LORD thy God bringeth thee into a good land, a land of brooks of water... a land of wheat, and barley, and vines, and fig trees... A land wherein thou shalt eat bread without scarceness, thou shalt not lack any thing in it...When thou hast eaten and art full, then thou shalt bless the LORD thy God for the good land which he hath given thee...

Beware that thou forget not the LORD thy God, in not keeping his commandments...Lest when thou hast eaten and art full, and hast built goodly houses, and dwelt therein...and thy silver and thy gold is multiplied, and all that thou hast is multiplied; Then thine heart be lifted up, and thou forget the LORD thy God... Who led thee... Who fed thee... And thou say in thine heart, My power and the might of mine hand hath gotten me this wealth.

But thou shalt remember the LORD thy God: for it is he that giveth thee power to get wealth, that he may establish his covenant (His Word and His work)...

6.   SONG: We Are Saying Thank You Jesus

We are saying thank you Jesus
Thank you my Lord
We are saying thank you Jesus
Thank you my Lord

We are saying thank you Jesus
Thank you my Lord
We are saying thank you Jesus
Thank you my Lord

7.   EXHORTATION (The scriptural exhortation should centre on the following):

i.   Thanking God for His divine provision.

ii. An admonition to the individual to remember God in the times of blessing.

8.   SONG: We Thank You Lord

We thank you Lord,
We thank you Lord
We thank you Jehovah Almighty

We thank you Lord,
We thank you Lord,
We thank you Jehovah Almighty

Author Unknown

9.   CLOSING PRAYER

10.   REFRESHMENTS

CHAPTER 6

Standard Wedding Ceremony

Therefore shall a man leave his father and his mother, and shall cleave unto his wife: and they shall be one flesh. And they were both naked, the man and his wife, and were not ashamed.

Genesis 2:24-25

1. **SONG: O Perfect Love** (Whilst Ministers file in and take their seats.)

O perfect Love,
All human thought transcending,
Lowly we kneel in prayer
before Thy throne,
That theirs may be,
the love which knows no ending
Whom Thou forevermore
dost join in one.

O perfect Life,
Be Thou their full assurance,
Of tender charity and steadfast faith,
Of patient hope
and quiet, brave endurance,
With childlike trust
that fears nor pain nor death.

By Dorothy F. Gurney (1883)

2. **BRIDAL MARCH** (Whilst bridal party files in.)

3. **WORSHIP TIME**

4. **INTRODUCTION** (Whilst at altar; couple stands, congregation sits.)

MINISTER: Dearly beloved, we are gathered here in the sight of God, and in the face of this congregation, to join together this man and this woman in Holy Matrimony, which is an honourable estate, instituted of God Himself, signifying unto us the mystical union that is betwixt Christ and His Church. Which Holy estate Christ adorned and beautified with His presence in the first miracle which He wrought in Cana of Galilee. And is commended in Holy writ to be honourable among all men, and therefore is not by any to be enterprised nor taken in hand unadvisedly, lightly or wantonly. But reverently, discreetly and soberly and in the fear of God, duly considering the causes for which matrimony was ordained.

FIRST, it was ordained for the increase of mankind according to the will of God, and that children might be brought up in the fear and nurture of the Lord, and to the praise of His Holy Name.

SECOND, it was ordained for a remedy against sin, and to avoid fornication; that such persons that have not the gift of self control might marry, and keep themselves undefiled members of Christ's body.

THIRD, it was ordained for mutual society help and comfort, that the one ought to have of the other both in prosperity and adversity. Into which Holy estate these two persons present, come now to be joined.

5. LEGAL CHARGE

MINISTER: I require and charge you both as you will answer at the day of judgement, when the secrets of all hearts will be disclosed, that if either of you know of any impediment why you may not be lawfully joined together in matrimony, ye do now confess it, for be ye well assured, that so many as are coupled together otherwise than God's Word doth allow, are not joined together by God, neither is their matrimony lawful.

MINISTER: (Bridegroom repeating after.) I do solemnly declare/ that I know not of any lawful impediment/ why I, ...(Name of bridegroom)... / may not be joined in matrimony to...(Name of bride)...

MINISTER: (Bride repeating after.) I do solemnly declare/ that I know not of any lawful impediment/ why I, ...(Name of bride)... / may not be joined in matrimony to ...(Name of bridegroom)....

6. "I WILL" VOWS

MINISTER: (To the Bridegroom.) ...(Name of bride-groom)..., wilt thou have this woman standing by your side to be thy wedded wife, to live together after God's ordinance, in the Holy estate of Matrimony; wilt thou love her, comfort her, honour and keep her, and forsaking all others, keep thee only unto her, so long as you both shall live?

GROOM: I certainly will.

MINISTER: (To the Bride.) ...(Name of bride)..., wilt thou have this man standing by your side to be thy wedded husband, to live together after God's ordinance in the Holy estate of Matrimony, wilt thou obey him and serve him, love, honour and keep him, and forsaking all other, keep thee only unto him, so long as you both shall live?

BRIDE: I certainly will.

7. GIVING AWAY OF BRIDE

MINISTER: Who giveth this woman to be married to this man? (Father stands, comes to the microphone)

FATHER: I, ...(Name of father)... on this ...(date)... do freely and willingly give away my daughter ...(Name of bride)..., in marriage, with all my blessings. (Father thanked and applauded by congregation.)

8. EXCHANGE OF VOWS (Minister instructs couple to face each other.)

MINISTER: (Bridegroom repeating after.) I, ...(Name of groom)... /according to the Word of God, / leave my father and my mother /and I join myself to you, / to be a husband to you. / From this moment forward, / I shall love you, / and I shall give myself to you, / and we shall be one.

MINISTER: (Bride repeating after.) I, ...(Name of bride)... / according to the Word of God, / submit myself to you, / to be a wife to you. / From this moment forward, / I shall love you, / and I shall give myself to you, / and we shall be one.

9. INTRODUCTION TO RING SERVICE

MINISTER: May I have the rings please.

These rings are precious ornaments, made out of pure gold. May the gold in these rings remind you of how pure your marriage shall be. These rings are given as a token and a symbol of your love and trust.

When you see these rings on your fingers, let them remind you of your love. Let them always remind you of the vows and promises you have made to each other this day.

Remember that real love is as strong as death and many waters cannot quench it, neither can the floods drown it. If anyone would break up this union, it would be Satan. Therefore give him no place. Give him no place. This marriage is forever.

Let us pray.

10. PRAYER OVER RINGS

MINISTER: In thy name O Lord, we hallow and dedicate these rings that by thy blessing, he who gives it and she who wears it keeping true faith for one to the other, may abide together in thy peace, continue together in thy favour, live together in thy love, and finally dwell together in thine eternal Kingdom through Jesus Christ our Lord. Amen.

11. EXCHANGE OF RINGS

MINISTER: (To Bridegroom whilst giving him Bride's ring.) I want you to place this ring on her finger with these things in mind. You are the Head of this union. This woman stands by your side, not at your feet.

I want her to wear this ring in remembrance that she is your help mate. It is not a symbol of domination but a reminder of love. So place this ring on her finger, and as you do, say this to her:

MINISTER: (Bridegroom repeating after.) ...(Mention first name of Bride three times).... With this ring,/ I thee wed./ I give it as a token of my faith./ I believe with all my heart/ that this marriage is forever./ It is all my love and all my faith,/ in the name of Jesus.

MINISTER: (To Bride whilst giving her Bridegroom's ring.) I want you to place this ring on his finger with these things in mind. This man is your Head. You have been called to help and support him.

Stand by him in all things, spiritually, physically and socially knowing that two are better than one. Now place this ring on his finger and as you do, say this to him.

MINISTER: (Bride repeating after.) ...(Mention first name of Bridegroom three times)....With this ring,/ I thee wed./ I give it as a token of my faith./ I believe with all my heart/ that this is forever./ It is my love, my sweet love,/ in the name of Jesus.

12. PRAYER AND LAYING ON OF HANDS (Bride and bridegroom kneel)

13. PRONOUNCEMENT OF MARRIAGE (Couple Stands.)

MINISTER: For as much as ...(Name of bridegroom)..., and ...(Name of bride)... have consented together in holy wedlock, and have witnessed the same before God and this company, and thereto have given and pledged their troth either to the other, and have declared the same by giving and receiving of rings, I pronounce that they be man and wife together in the name of the Father and of the Son and of the Holy Ghost. Amen.

14. SONG: In His Time He Makes All Things Beautiful

In His time, in His time
He makes all things beautiful
in His time
Lord please show me everyday
As you're teaching me your way
That you do just what you say
in your time

In Your time, in Your time
You make all things beautiful
in your time
Lord my life to you I bring
May each song I have to sing
Be to you a lovely thing,
in your time

By Maranatha Music

15. REMOVAL OF VEIL AND SALUTATION OF BRIDE [Ask the Bridegroom to remove the Bride's veil and salute (kiss) his Bride.]

16. COMMUNION

MINISTER: The couple will now receive Communion together. Hitherto they have come to the Lord's Table as separate individuals but now they come as one flesh. The celebration of communion is to remind us all that it is because of what Christ has done for us that we are here in the first place. The Lord Jesus the same night in which he was betrayed took bread, and when he had given thanks broke it and said, take, eat, this is my body which is broken for you. This do in remembrance of me. After the same manner also he took the cup, when he had supped, saying, this cup is the new testament in my blood. This do ye, as oft as ye drink in remembrance of me. For as often as ye eat this bread and drink this cup, ye do show the Lord's death till He come.

Let us pray. (Bless the bread and the wine. Thank God for Jesus Christ's sacrifice.)

17. SONG: Love Divine

Love Divine, all loves excelling,
Joy of heaven, to earth come down,
Fix in us thy humble dwelling,
All thy faithful mercies crown.
Jesus, thou art all compassion,
Pure unbounded love thou art;
Visit us with thy salvation,
Enter every trembling heart.

Come, almighty to deliver,
Let us all thy grace receive;
Suddenly return, and never,
Never more thy temples leave.
Thee we would be always blessing,
Serve thee as thy hosts above,
Pray, and praise thee, without ceasing,
Glory in thy perfect love

By Charles Wesley (1747)

18. SIGNING OF REGISTER & OFFERING

19. SCRIPTURE READINGS

Genesis 2:18-25

And the LORD God said, It is not good that the man should be alone; I will make him an help meet for him. And out of the ground the LORD God formed every beast of the field, and every fowl of the air; and brought them unto Adam to see what he would call them: and whatsoever Adam called every living creature, that was the name thereof.

And Adam gave names to all cattle, and to the fowl of the air, and to every beast of the field; but for Adam there was not found an help meet for him. And the LORD God caused a deep sleep to fall upon Adam, and he slept: and he took one of his ribs, and closed up the flesh instead thereof; And the rib, which the LORD God had taken from man, made he a woman, and brought her unto the man.

And Adam said, This is now bone of my bones, and flesh of my flesh: she shall be called Woman, because she was taken out of Man. Therefore shall a man leave his father and his mother, and shall cleave unto his wife: and they shall be one flesh. And they were both naked, the man and his wife, and were not ashamed.

Ephesians 5:20-33

Giving thanks always for all things unto God and the Father in the name of our Lord Jesus Christ; Submitting yourselves one to another in the fear of God. Wives, submit yourselves unto your own husbands, as unto the Lord. For the husband is the head of the wife, even as Christ is the head of the church: and he is the saviour of the body. Therefore as the church is subject unto Christ, so let the wives be to their own husbands in every thing.

Husbands, love your wives, even as Christ also loved the church, and gave himself for it; That he might sanctify and cleanse it with the washing of water by the word, That he might present it to himself a glorious church, not having spot, or wrinkle, or any such thing; but that it should be holy and without blemish. So ought men to love their wives as their own bodies. He that loveth his wife loveth himself. For no man ever yet hated his own flesh; but nourisheth and cherisheth it, even as the Lord the church: For we are members of his body, of his flesh, and of his bones. For this cause shall a man leave his father and mother, and shall be joined unto his wife, and they two shall be one flesh. This is a great mystery: but I speak concerning Christ and the church.

Nevertheless let every one of you in particular so love his wife even as himself; and the wife see that she reverence her husband.

20. **SERMON**

21. **CHARGE AND BLESSING** (Couple stands, congregation sits.)

MINISTER: I now charge you in the presence of God Almighty that you trust in the Lord with all your heart. Lean not on your own insight. In all your ways acknowledge him. And He will direct your paths.

These blessings will come on you and overtake you, if you will hearken unto the voice of the Lord your God.

Blessed shall thou be in the city, and blessed shalt thou be in the field.

Blessed shall be the fruit of thy body. Blessed shall be thy basket and thy store.

Blessed shall thou be when thou cometh in, and blessed shall thou be when thou goest out.

The Lord shall cause thine enemies that rise up against thee to be smitten before thy face: they shall come out against thee one way, and flee before thee seven ways.

The Lord shall command the blessing upon all that thou settest thine hand unto. The Lord shall establish thee an holy people unto himself.

And the Lord shall make thee plenteous in goods, in the fruit of thy body. And thou shalt lend unto many and thou shalt not borrow.

And the Lord shall make thee the head, and not the tail; and thou shalt be above only and thou shalt not be beneath; if that thou hearken unto the commandments of the Lord thy God.

22. PRAYER OF BLESSING

23. PRESENTATION TO CONGREGATION

MINISTER: (To Bride & Groom) Please turn and face this congregation.

MINISTER: (To Congregation) Ladies and gentlemen, I present to you Dr./Mr./Rev./Pastor/etc. and Mrs./ Dr. Mrs. ...(Last name of bridegroom)...

24. WEDDING MARCH

25. COUPLE FILES OUT (Followed by officiating ministers, then families.)

CHAPTER 7

Concise Wedding Ceremony

This ceremony is intended to take a shorter time than the standard wedding ceremony. It also presents an alternative set of vows, promises and proclamations. There are times when the couple may be late in arriving and a shorter ceremony may be more apt. There may also be mitigating circumstances which may make it necessary to have a short ceremony. Use this set of vows as the occasion demands.

1. **SONG: O Perfect Love** (Whilst Ministers file in and take their seats.)

O perfect Love,
All human thought transcending,
Lowly we kneel in prayer
before Thy throne,
That theirs may be,
the love which knows no ending
Whom Thou forevermore
dost join in one.

O perfect Life,
Be Thou their full assurance,
Of tender charity and steadfast faith,
Of patient hope
and quiet, brave endurance,
With childlike trust
that fears nor pain nor death.
By Dorothy F. Gurney (1883)

2. **BRIDAL MARCH (Whilst bridal party files in.)**

3. **PRAISE & WORSHIP**

4. **INTRODUCTION** (Whilst at altar; couple stands, congregation sits.)

MINISTER: Dearly beloved, we are gathered here in the sight of God, and in the face of this congregation, to join together this man and this woman in Holy Matrimony, which is commended of the Apostle Paul to be honourable among all men, into which Holy estate these two come now to be joined.

5. **LEGAL CHARGE**

MINISTER: I require and charge you both that if you know of any just cause why you may not marry, you should, with all sincerity say so now, not forgetting that any two coupled together in contradiction to the Word of God are not joined together by God, neither is such matrimony lawful.

MINISTER: (Bridegroom repeating after.) I solemnly declare/ that I do not know of any lawful impediment/ why I ...(Name of bridegroom)... / may not be joined in matrimony to ...(Name of bride)....

33

MINISTER: (Bride repeating after.) I solemnly declare/ that I do not know of any lawful impediment/ why I ...(Name of bride)... / may not be joined in matrimony to ...(Name of bridegroom)....

6.   "I DO" VOWS

MINISTER: (To Bridegroom.)   ...(Name of bridegroom)..., do you love ...(Name of bride)... and do you receive her now to be your wedded wife? Do you promise to honour and cherish her and forsaking all others, cleave only unto her as long as both of you shall live?

GROOM: I do

MINISTER: (To Bride.)   ...(Name of bride)..., do you love ...(Name of bridegroom)... and do you receive him now to be your wedded husband? Do you promise to obey, honour and cherish him and forsaking all others, cleave only unto him as long as both of you shall live?

BRIDE: I do

7.   GIVING AWAY OF BRIDE

MINISTER: Who gives the bride away into marriage?

BRIDE'S FATHER: I do

8.   EXCHANGE OF VOWS (Instruct couple to face each other.)

MINISTER: (Bridegroom repeating after.)   I, ...(Name of bridegroom)..., / according to the Word of God, / leave my father and my mother / and I join myself to you, / to be a husband to you. / From this moment forward, / we shall be one.

MINISTER: (Bride repeating after.) I, ...(Name of bride)..., / according to the Word of God, / submit myself to you, / to be a wife to you. / From this moment forward, / we shall be one.

9. INTRODUCTION TO RING SERVICE

MINISTER: Made of gold, one of the purest metals, the ring suggests your commitment to unfailing purity and fidelity in your marriage. As you wear it, may you be continually reminded of this commitment. Also, a ring is a complete circle with no point of division. This demonstrates a commitment on your part to remain unseparated for the rest of your lives.

10. PRAYER OVER RINGS

MINISTER: Father, we ask you to redeem these rings with the blood of Jesus, and bless them, that as they wear them, it will be a promise to keep their vows as long as they live. In Jesus' name.

11. EXCHANGE OF RINGS (Presents ring to Bridegroom.)

MINISTER: (Bridegroom repeating after. Mention first name of Bride three times) ...(Name of bride)....With this ring / I commit all my love to you. / As I love the Lord, / so do I love you. / I receive you as God's gift to me. / As God enables me, / I will lead our home spiritually, / physically / and socially / under the Lordship of Jesus Christ. / I will seek to support and encourage you / through each challenge of life. / All that is mine is yours / until death shall part us.

(Minister presents ring to the Bride.)

MINISTER: (Bride repeating after. Mention first name of Bridegroom three times). ...(Name of bridegroom).... With this ring / I commit all my love to you. / As I love the Lord, / so do I love you. / I receive you as God's gift to me. / I trust the Lord / to enable me to be submissive to you / as my spiritual head/ and leader of our home. /

I will seek to support / and encourage you / spiritually, / physically / and socially / through each challenge of life. / All that is mine is yours / until death shall part us.

12. **PRAYER, AND LAYING ON OF HANDS:** (Bride and bridegroom kneel)

13. **PRONOUNCEMENT OF MARRIAGE** (Couple stands.)

MINISTER: For as much as ...(Name of bridegroom)..., and ...(Name of bride)... have openly declared their intention before God and this congregation, to keep all the vows they have made to each other today, it is my privilege as a minister of the gospel and by the authority vested in me by the Lord Jesus Christ, to pronounce from this day forward: You are husband and wife. Amen

14. **REMOVAL OF VEIL & SALUTATION** (Minister asks Bridegroom to remove veil and kiss his Bride).

15. **SONG: Love Divine**

Love Divine, all loves excelling,
Joy of heaven, to earth come down,
Fix in us thy humble dwelling,
All thy faithful mercies crown.
Jesus, thou art all compassion,
Pure unbounded love thou art;
Visit us with thy salvation,
Enter every trembling heart.

Come, almighty to deliver,
Let us all thy grace receive;
Suddenly return, and never,
Never more thy temples leave.
Thee we would be always blessing,
Serve thee as thy hosts above,
Pray, and praise thee, without ceasing,
Glory in thy perfect love

By Charles Wesley (1747)

16.   SIGNING OF REGISTER & OFFERING

17.   SCRIPTURE READING

Genesis 2:18-25

And the LORD God said, It is not good that the man should be alone; I will make him an help meet for him. And out of the ground the LORD God formed every beast of the field, and every fowl of the air; and brought them unto Adam to see what he would call them: and whatsoever Adam called every living creature, that was the name thereof. And Adam gave names to all cattle, and to the fowl of the air, and to every beast of the field; but for Adam there was not found an help meet for him. And the LORD God caused a deep sleep to fall upon Adam, and he slept: and he took one of his ribs, and closed up the flesh instead thereof;

And the rib, which the LORD God had taken from man, made he a woman, and brought her unto the man. And Adam said, This is now bone of my bones, and flesh of my flesh: she shall be called Woman, because she was taken out of Man. Therefore shall a man leave his father and his mother, and shall cleave unto his wife: and they shall be one flesh. And they were both naked, the man and his wife, and were not ashamed.

18.   SERMON

19.   CHARGE AND BLESSING

MINISTER: (Couple stands, congregation sits.)   May the Lord bless you with the dew of heaven and the good things of above. May He bless you with the fatness of the earth, the corn, the oil, and the wine.

May the Lord bless you, multiply you and make you great in the land.

May your horn be exalted like the horn of the unicorn and may your marriage always be anointed with fresh oil. Be planted in the House of the Lord and flourish in the courts of our God.

In the name of the Father, the Son, and the Holy Ghost. Amen.

20. PRESENTATION TO CONGREGATION

MINISTER: (To Bride & Groom) Please turn and face this congregation.

MINISTER: (To Congregation) Ladies and gentlemen, I present to you Mr. and Mrs. ...(Last name of bridegroom)....

21. WEDDING MARCH

CHAPTER 8

Blessing a Wedding in the Church Office

Some couples encounter circumstances which do not allow them to have a full-blown wedding ceremony in the church. For instance, there may be financial hindrances preventing a regular wedding ceremony at the time. Also, publicly known immorality and pregnancies may necessitate such an event. Some couples also prefer a quieter ceremony.

It is under such circumstances that you may have to use this set of vows.

This ceremony is a little different from the regular ones as the couple may wish to have a Standard Wedding Ceremony later on. This ceremony is held in the church office and must be brief.

1. OPENING PRAYER

2. SONG: To God Be the Glory

	Chorus:
To God be the glory,	*Praise the Lord! Praise the Lord!*
Great things He hath done	*Let the earth hear His voice*
So loved He the world that	*Praise the Lord! Praise the Lord,*
He gave us His Son	*Let the people rejoice*
Who yielded His life	*O come to the Father*
An atonement for sin	*through Jesus the Son*
And opened the life gate	*And give Him the glory great things*
that all may go in	*He hath done*

By Fanny Crossby (1875)

3. INTRODUCTION (Couple stands, and witnesses sit.)

MINISTER: We are assembled today under the banner of the Lord to bless this marriage. The steps of a good man are ordered by the Lord and He delighteth in his way. Except the Lord build the house, we know that we build in vain. We therefore, come before the Lord at this time:

i. To acknowledge Him in this marriage as the Giver of all good things.

ii. To fulfil all righteousness as required by the laws of the land and the Church.

iii. To ask the Lord for His hand, His favour, and His blessing upon the marriage between ...(Name of bridegroom)... and ...(Name of bride)....

4. LEGAL CHARGE

MINISTER: I require and charge you both that if you know of any just cause why you may not be legally married, you should, with all sincerity say so now, not forgetting that any two coupled together in contradiction to the Word of God are not joined together by God neither is such matrimony lawful.

MINISTER: (Bridegroom repeating after.) I solemnly declare / that I do not know of any lawful impediment / why I ...(Name of bridegroom)... / may not be joined in matrimony to / ...(Name of bride)....

MINISTER: (Bride repeating after.) I solemnly declare / that I do not know of any lawful impediment / why I ...(Name of bride)... / may not be joined in matrimony to / ...(Name of bridegroom)....

5. "I DO" VOWS

MINISTER: (To Bridegroom.) ...(Name of bridegroom)..., do you, before God and all these witnesses choose ...(Name of bride)... as your wedded wife? And do you promise to love her as Christ loved the church and give yourself for her as long as you live?

GROOM: I do

MINISTER: (To Bride.) ...(Name of bride)..., do you, before God and all these witnesses choose ...(Name of bridegroom)... as your wedded husband? And do you promise to submit yourself to him as unto the Lord and love him as long as you live?

BRIDE: I do

6. GIVING AWAY OF BRIDE

MINISTER: Who gives the bride away into marriage to this man?

BRIDE'S FATHER: I do

7. EXCHANGE OF VOWS (Instruct couple to face each other)

MINISTER: (Ask Bridegroom to repeat) I, ...(Name of bridegroom)..., / take you, ...(Name of bride)... / to be my wedded wife; / to have and to hold

/ from this day forward. / To care for and to encourage, / in prosperity and adversity. / I promise to live for Christ. / I promise to love and trust you forever. / And with this commitment, / I pledge to you my life.

MINISTER: (Ask Bride to repeat) I, ...(Name of bride)..., / take you, ...(Name of bridegroom)... / to be my wedded husband; / to have and to hold / from this day forward. / To care for and to encourage, / in prosperity and adversity. / I promise to live for Christ. / I promise to love and trust you forever. / And with this commitment, / I pledge to you my life.

8.   INTRODUCTION TO RING SERVICE

MINISTER: May I have the rings please? These rings are symbols of your commitment of love. They are made out of gold, expressing the purity that should always be in your marriage. You are going to exchange these rings in full awareness of the deep implications thereof.

9   PRAYER OVER RINGS

MINISTER: Lord, we dedicate and sanctify these rings today. May they be symbols of true love and tokens of commitment between these two. Bless these rings now in the name of Jesus. Amen.

10.   EXCHANGE OF RINGS

MINISTER: (Present ring to Bridegroom and ask him to repeat) I give this ring / as a visible token of my love. / I give it to you / as a visible token / of my permanent commitment / and dedication to you. / From today I am yours / and you are mine. / I love you with all my heart/ and I will always love you. / In the name of Jesus. Amen.

MINISTER: (Presents ring to Bride and ask her to repeat) I give this ring / as a visible token of my love / and I give it to you / as my own life. / From today, I am yours / and you are mine / I love you with all my heart / and I will always love you. / In the name of the Lord Jesus. Amen.

11. **PRAYER, AND LAYING ON OF HANDS:** (Bride and bridegroom kneel)

12. **PRONOUNCEMENT OF MARRIAGE** (Couple stands)

MINISTER: For as much as...(Name of bridegroom)..., and ...(Name of bride)... have openly declared their intention to keep all the vows they have made to each other today, it is my privilege as a minister of the gospel and by the authority vested in me by the Lord Jesus Christ to pronounce from this day forward, that your marriage is blessed by the Lord and you are husband and wife before man and before God. In the name of the Father, the Son, and the Holy Ghost. Amen.

13. **BRIDEGROOM SALUTES BRIDE** (Ask the Bridegroom to kiss his Bride)

14. **HYMN 2: O Perfect Love**

O perfect Love,
All human thought transcending,
Lowly we kneel in prayer
before Thy throne,
That theirs may be,
  the love which knows no ending
Whom Thou forevermore

dost join in one.

O perfect Life,
Be Thou their full assurance,
Of tender charity and steadfast faith,
Of patient hope
 and quiet, brave endurance,
With childlike trust
that fears nor pain nor death.

                By Dorothy F. Gurney (1883)

15. **SIGNING OF REGISTER/OFFERING**

16. **BIBLE READING: (Optional)**

Genesis 2:18-25

And the LORD God said, It is not good that the man should be alone; I will make him an help meet for him. And out of the ground the LORD God formed every beast of the field, and every fowl of the air; and brought them unto Adam to see what he would call them: and whatsoever Adam called every living creature, that was the name thereof. And Adam gave names to all cattle, and to the fowl of the air, and to every beast of the field; but for Adam there was not found an help meet for him.

And the LORD God caused a deep sleep to fall upon Adam, and he slept: and he took one of his ribs, and closed up the flesh instead thereof; And the rib, which the LORD God had taken from man, made he a woman, and brought her unto the man. And Adam said, This is now bone of my bones, and flesh of my flesh: she shall be called Woman, because she was taken out of Man. Therefore shall a man leave his father and his mother, and shall cleave unto his wife: and they shall be one flesh. And they were both naked, the man and his wife, and were not ashamed.

17. **SERMON**

18. **CHARGE AND BLESSING** (Couple stands, witnesses sit)

MINISTER: I want to speak a word of blessing and exhortation to you, as you move on as husband and wife.

You shall be like a tree planted by the rivers of water, and you shall bring forth your fruit in its season.

Your leaves shall not whither, and whatsoever you do shall prosper, if you shall hearken unto the voice of the Lord. Be a husband and wife that walk not in the counsel of ungodly people.

He is your glory and He shall be the lifter of your head. At thy latter end the Lord shall enlarge thee and shall have mercy upon thee.

Though thy beginnings be small, thy latter end shall be greatly increased. In the name of the Father, the Son, and the Holy Ghost. Amen.

19. PRAYER OF BLESSING

20. HYMN 3: Great is Thy Faithfulness

Great is thy faithfulness,
O Lord my Father
There is no shadow of turning with Thee
Thou changest not,
* thy compassions they fail not*
As thou hast been thou forever will be

Chorus
Great is thy faithfulness,
great is thy faithfulness
Morning by morning
* new mercies I see*
All I have needed
Thy hand hath provided
Great is Thy faithfulness,
Lord, unto me

By Thomas Chrisholm

21. PRESENTATION TO WITNESSES

MINISTER: (To Bride and Groom:) Please turn and face the witnesses herein gathered.

MINISTER: (To Witnesses:) Ladies and gentlemen, I present to you Mr. and Mrs. ...(Last name of bridegroom)....

22. COUPLE RECESS

MINISTER: Shall we sing as they march out.

23. HYMN 4: How Great Thou Art

O Lord my God, When I in awesome wonder
Consider all the worlds thy hand has made
I see the stars, I hear the roaring thunder
Thy power throughout the universe displayed

Chorus
Then sings my soul,
My Saviour God to thee
How great thou art
How great thou art

By Carl Boberg,
Translated by Stuart K Kine (1949)

45

CHAPTER 9

Blessing a Marriage
At Home

And the Lord God said, It is not good that the man
should be alone; I will make him an help meet for him.

Genesis 2:18

1. **OFFICIATING MINISTER PRAYS OVER RING**
    (Prior to it being placed on woman's finger at the
    engagement.)

2. **OPENING PRAYER FOR BLESSING CEREMONY**

3. **SONG: To God Be the Glory**

To God be the glory,
Great things He hath done
So loved He the world that
He gave us His Son
Who yielded His life
An atonement for sin
And opened the life gate
that all may go in

Chorus:
Praise the Lord! Praise the Lord!
Let the earth hear His voice
Praise the Lord! Praise the Lord,
Let the people rejoice
O come to the Father
through Jesus the Son
And give Him the glory great things
He hath done

By Fanny Crossby (1875)

4. **REASON FOR OCCASION**

MINISTER: We want, at this time, to acknowledge the Lord
especially in this marriage being established
today.

According to the Word of God, ...(Name of
bridegroom)... and ...(Name of bride)... have
given tribute to whom tribute is due, custom
to whom custom is due, and honour to whom
honour is due.

We come at this time to acknowledge the hand of
the Lord God Jehovah in all things. If the Lord
doth not build the house we labour in vain. We
therefore ask the Lord to build this house.

5. **SCRIPTURE READING**

Genesis 2:18-25

And the LORD God said, It is not good that the man should
be alone; I will make him an help meet for him. And out of

the ground the LORD God formed every beast of the field, and every fowl of the air; and brought them unto Adam to see what he would call them: and whatsoever Adam called every living creature, that was the name thereof. And Adam gave names to all cattle, and to the fowl of the air, and to every beast of the field; but for Adam there was not found an help meet for him.

And the LORD God caused a deep sleep to fall upon Adam, and he slept: and he took one of his ribs, and closed up the flesh instead thereof; And the rib, which the LORD God had taken from man, made he a woman, and brought her unto the man. And Adam said, This is now bone of my bones, and flesh of my flesh: she shall be called Woman, because she was taken out of Man. Therefore shall a man leave his father and his mother, and shall cleave unto his wife: and they shall be one flesh. And they were both naked, the man and his wife, and were not ashamed.

6.   SERMON / EXHORTATION

7.   EXCHANGE OF VOWS (Couple facing each other.)

MINISTER: (Bridegroom repeating after.)   I, ...(Name of bridegroom)..., / take you ...(Name of bride)... / to be my cherished wife / I promise you with all my heart / to walk beside you/ in times of happiness / and in times of great adversity. / I commit my love to you / and I promise to be faithful to you / and to you alone / until Christ comes. / In the name of the Father, / the Son, / and the Holy Ghost. / Amen.

MINISTER: (Bride repeating after.)   I ...(Name of bride)..., / take you ...(Name of bridegroom)... / to be my cherished husband. / I promise you with all my heart/ to walk beside you/ in times of adversity/ and in times of great happiness./ I commit my love to you/ and I promise to be faithful to you/ and to you alone/ until Christ comes again./ In

the name of the Father,/ the Son,/ and the Holy
Ghost./ Amen.

8.   **PRAYER OF BLESSING** (Couple kneel)

MINISTER: The Lord bless thee, and keep thee: The Lord
make his face shine upon thee, and be gracious
unto thee: The Lord lift up his countenance upon
thee, and give thee peace.

In the name of Jesus.

9.   **PRONOUNCEMENT OF MARRIAGE** (Couple
stands.)

MINISTER: Today, ...(Name of bridegroom)... and ...(Name of
bride)... have fulfiled all customary requirements
and have also submitted their marriage to the
Blessing of the Lord. I stand as a Minister of the
Lord Jesus Christ to pronounce that this marriage
is indeed blessed and sanctified of the Lord. And
what God has put together, let no man or woman
put asunder.

In the name of the Father, the Son, and the Holy
Ghost. Amen.

10. **SALUTATION OF BRIDE** (Ask Bridegroom to kiss
his Bride)

11. **SONG: Showers of Blessing**

There shall be showers of blessing;
This is the promise of God
There shall be seasons refreshing,
Sent from the Saviour above

Chorus
Showers of blessing,
Showers of blessing we plead
Mercy drops round us are
falling,
But for the showers we plead

By Daniel W. Whittle (1883)

12. **CLOSING PRAYER**

CHAPTER 10

Renewal of Vows

This ceremony is performed by couples who wish to celebrate a longstanding marriage which has passed through the tests of time. As ministers we are servants of the Lord. If they wish to engage in an elaborate anniversary celebration of what the Lord has done for them, it is only appropriate to flow along and support them. Minister to them and speak the blessings of the Lord upon them that they may continue in happiness for many more years.

The vows in this section have been specially formulated to suit such an occasion.

1.   SONG: To God Be the Glory

Chorus:

To God be the glory,	*Praise the Lord! Praise the Lord!*
Great things He hath done	*Let the earth hear His voice*
So loved He the world that	*Praise the Lord! Praise the Lord,*
He gave us His Son	*Let the people rejoice*
Who yielded His life	*O come to the Father*
An atonement for sin	*through Jesus the Son*
And opened the life gate	*And give Him the glory great things*
that all may go in	*He hath done*

By Fanny Crossby (1875)

2.   BRIDAL MARCH

3.   WORSHIP

4.   INTRODUCTION (Whilst at altar, couple stands and congregation sits.)

MINISTER: Dearly beloved, we come to this house of worship to celebrate together the marriage of Mr. and Mrs. ...(Last name of the bridegroom)....

Marriage is honourable and it is fitting and proper that this marriage ceremony be celebrated in the presence of God.

God sanctified marriage when He brought together the first man and the first woman.

The Lord Jesus hallowed the occasion of marriage by His presence in His first miracle which He wrought in Cana of Galilee.

The Word of God teaches and speaks of the honour, the correctness, the sanctity, the holiness, and the blessedness of marriage.

All these are the portion of Christians who come to the marriage altar desiring to have a blessed and happy marriage.

The nearest place to heaven in this world is a Christ centred home. The nearest place to hell on earth is a house where hatred, bitterness, and quarrels prevail. Except the Lord build a home of love, peace, and joy in the Holy Ghost we know that we build in vain.

It is for this reason that these two persons come again to renew and affirm their love and commitment to this Holy estate of matrimony.

5. "I DO" VOWS

MINISTER: (To the Bridegroom.)   ...(Name of bridegroom)..., do you affirm your unconditional love and commitment to ...(Name of bride)...? Do you promise to continue living together after God's ordinance in the Holy estate of matrimony; will you encourage her, honour and keep her, and not allow any circumstance to affect your faithfulness to her, so long as you both shall live?

GROOM: I do

MINISTER: (To the Bride.) ...(Name of bride)..., do you affirm your unconditional love, submission and commitment to ...(Name of bridegroom)...? Do you promise to continue living together after God's ordinance in the Holy estate of matrimony; will you encourage him, honour and keep him, and not allow any circumstance to affect your faithfulness to him, so long as you both shall live?

BRIDE: I do

6. DECLARATION OF WITNESS

MINISTER: Who stands as a witness to this renewal of vows between the couple?

(Witness stands, comes forward to the microphone)

WITNESS: I, ...(Name of father)..., confirm that I have freely and willingly given away my daughter in marriage with all my blessings.

OR

WITNESS: I ...(Name of witness)..., confirm that I have witnessed the renewal of marriage between Mr. and Mrs. ...(Last name of the couple)... in the House of God.

7.   RENEWAL OF VOWS (Couple facing each other.)

MINISTER: (Bridegroom repeating after.) I, ...(Name of bridegroom)..., / having chosen you among all / and having married you, / this day renew my vows to you that; / I will offer myself completely to you / as your wedded husband. / I promise to love you with all my heart/ and to be faithful. / I promise to stand by you always, / in times of joy, / in times of trials / and in times of sorrow. / I dedicate our marriage and our home / to the Lordship of Jesus Christ. / I pledge myself / and all that I am/ to this eternal covenant. / So help me God.

MINISTER: (Bride repeating after.) I, ...(Name of bride)... / having chosen you among all / and having married you / this day renew my vows to you that; / In response to your love for me, / I will offer myself / in the beauty of submission / to you as your wife / I also promise to love you / with all my heart/ and to be faithful./

I promise to stand by you always, / in times of joy, / in times of trial / and in times of sorrow / I pledge myself / and all that I am / to this eternal covenant./ So help me God.

8. INTRODUCTION OF RING SERVICE

MINISTER: These rings are very precious and special. Today, we renew their purpose. Let them remain forever as a symbol of your love and commitment towards each other. Shall we pray.

9. PRAYER OVER RINGS

MINISTER: Father, we ask you to redeem these rings once again with the blood of Jesus, and bless this couple with a fresh blessing that their love may be renewed as they wear them. Let them be a sign that these two shall by your grace keep their vows as long as they live. In Jesus' name.

10. EXCHANGE OF RINGS (Present ring to Bridegroom followed by him repeating the vows then present ring to Bride followed by her repeating the vows)

MINISTER: (Bridegroom repeating after.) (Mention first name of Bride three times) ...(Name of bride)..., / this ring is an expression / of all I have promised you. / I give it with all my love / and life-long commitment. / In the name of the Father, / the Son, / and the Holy Spirit. / Amen

MINISTER: (Bride repeating after.) (Mention first name of Bridegroom three times). ...(Name of bridegroom)..., / this ring is an expression / of all I have promised you. / I give it with all my love / and life-long commitment. / In the name of the Father, / the Son, / and the Holy Spirit. / Amen.

11. PRAYER, AND LAYING ON OF HANDS: (Bride and bridegroom kneel.)

12. PRONOUNCEMENT OF MARRIAGE (Couple stands.)

MINISTER: For as much as Mr. and Mrs. ...(Last name of bridegroom)..., have openly renewed their vows to God and to each other today, and have declared their intention to keep and maintain this marriage, it is my privilege as a minister of the gospel and by the authority vested in me by the Lord Jesus Christ to pronounce that you are husband and wife afresh, in the name of the Father, the Son and the Holy Ghost. Amen.

13. **SALUTATION OF BRIDE** [Ask Bridegroom to salute (kiss) his Bride]

14. **COMMUNION**

MINISTER: The couple will now receive Communion together. This is to remind us all that it is because of what Christ has done for us that we are all here in the first place. The Lord Jesus the same night in which he was betrayed took bread, and when he had given thanks he brake it and said take, eat, this is my body which is broken for you. This do in remembrance of me.

After the same manner also he took the cup, when he had supped, saying, this cup is the new testament in my blood. This do ye, as oft as ye drink in remembrance of me. For as often as ye eat this bread and drink this cup, ye do show the Lord's death till he come.

Let us pray. (Bless the bread and the wine. Thank God for Jesus Christ's sacrifice.)

15. **SCRIPTURE READINGS**

Genesis 2:18-25

And the LORD God said, It is not good that the man should be alone; I will make him an help meet for him. And out of the ground the LORD God formed every beast of the field, and every fowl of the air; and brought them unto Adam to see what he would call them: and whatsoever Adam called every living creature, that was the name thereof. And Adam gave names to all cattle, and to the fowl of the air, and to every beast of the field; but for Adam there was not found an help meet for him.

And the LORD God caused a deep sleep to fall upon Adam, and he slept: and he took one of his ribs, and closed up the flesh instead thereof; And the rib, which the LORD God had taken from man, made he a woman, and brought her unto the man. And Adam said, This is now bone of my bones, and flesh of my flesh: she shall be called Woman, because she was taken out of Man. Therefore shall a man leave his father and his mother, and shall cleave unto his wife: and they shall be one flesh. And they were both naked, the man and his wife, and were not ashamed.

Ephesians 5:20-33

Giving thanks always for all things unto God and the Father in the name of our Lord Jesus Christ; Submitting yourselves one to another in the fear of God. Wives, submit yourselves unto your own husbands, as unto the Lord. For the husband is the head of the wife, even as Christ is the head of the church: and he is the saviour of the body.

Therefore as the church is subject unto Christ, so let the wives be to their own husbands in every thing. Husbands, love your wives, even as Christ also loved the church, and gave himself for it; That he might sanctify and cleanse it with the washing of water by the word, That he might present it to himself a glorious church, not having spot, or wrinkle, or any such thing; but that it should be holy and without blemish. So ought men to love their wives as their own bodies. He that loveth his wife loveth himself.

*For no man ever yet hated his own flesh; but nourisheth
and cherisheth it, even as the Lord the church: For we are
members of his body, of his flesh, and of his bones. For this
cause shall a man leave his father and mother, and shall
be joined unto his wife, and they two shall be one flesh.
This is a great mystery: but I speak concerning Christ and
the church. Nevertheless let every one of you in particular
so love his wife even as himself; and the wife see that she
reverence her husband.*

16. SERMON

17. CHARGE AND BLESSING (Couple stands, congregation sits.)

MINISTER: Trust in the Lord and do good, and He shall cause you to be established in the land and He shall provide for you.

Delight yourself in the Lord and He shall give you the desires of your heart. Commit your ways unto the Lord and trust him and He shall bring it to pass.

I bring down the walls of opposition and resistance that are lifted up against your life and your peace. I reverse, I nullify, I cancel, and I reject every unscriptural prayer and death wish against your life.

I resist the desire of the enemy to see your downfall. I superimpose the will of God over and against every setback, every limitation, and every disappointment of your life.

May your lives be extended. May your days be prolonged. May the rest of your years together be sweeter and better then the ones that are passed. May the blessing of God replace every curse.

> May a new day dawn upon your horizon. And may the goodness and favour of the Lord shine upon you in the name of the Father, the Son, and the Holy Ghost. Amen.

18. PRAYER OF BLESSING

19. PRESENTATION TO CONGREGATION

MINISTER: (To Bride and Groom.) Please turn and face this congregation.

MINISTER: (To Congregation.) Ladies and gentlemen, I present to you Mr. and Mrs. ...(Last name of bridegroom)...

20. WEDDING MARCH

CHAPTER 11

Wake-Keeping Service

Many families lay the body of the deceased in state for a period. This is an important and sorrowful occasion for all families. It is necessary that the pastor is present to introduce a spiritual and encouraging mood into a usually depressed atmosphere. The presence of a choir singing praises to God is a very helpful addition to the service.

1. **OPENING PRAYER**

2. **PURPOSE**

   MINISTER: Dear brethren, the Word of God instructs us to rejoice with them that do rejoice and to mourn with them that mourn.

   As a church, we are also a family and consider our late ...(Name of deceased)... not just as a member of our church but as our brother/sister/father/mother. We really feel the loss together.

   But as it is written, all things work together for good to them that love the Lord. In all things we must give thanks, for this is the will of God.

   Tonight we come here to mourn with you all and also to comfort ourselves through our fellowship with the Holy Spirit.

   Shall we bow our heads in prayer.

3. **PRAISE AND WORSHIP**

4. **FILING PAST THE BODY** (with choir music/special songs)

5. **EXHORTATION / PREACHING**

6. **ALTAR CALL**

7. **SPECIAL SONG**

8. **ANNOUNCEMENTS**

9. **CLOSING PRAYER**

CHAPTER 12

Funeral Service

The Funeral Service may be held at the home of the deceased or in his church. However, some congregations meet in places which cannot be used as venues for funeral services. The pastor must therefore be flexible, and flow with whatever is appropriate.

The pastor must minister with a spirit of hope and encouragement. It is important to note that the family is already sad and depressed. There is therefore no need to deepen their sorrow any further.

However, it is an appropriate occasion to minister to people on the reality of heaven or hell and the need to be genuinely 'born again'. Every minister of God must use this opportunity to preach the Word of God to people who may otherwise never hear the Gospel. An altar call for salvation is most appropriate, and must be made at every funeral service.

1. **CONGREGATION PAYS LAST RESPECTS**

2. **OFFICIATING MINISTERS ENTER, FILE PAST THE CORPSE AND TAKE THEIR SEATS**

3. **COFFIN IS CLOSED FINALLY**

4. **CONGREGATION STANDS**

5. **SONG: Lead Us Heavenly Father**

Lead us heavenly Father lead us
O'er the world's tempestuous sea
Guard us, guide us, keep us, feed us
For we have no help but Thee,
Yet possessing every blessing
If our God our Father be

Saviour breathe forgiveness O'er us
All our weakness Thou dost know
Thou didst tread this earth before us
Thou didst feel its keenest woe
Lone and dreary, faint and weary
Through the desert Thou didst go

By James Ednesto

6. **OPENING PRAYER**

7. **FIRST SCRIPTURE READING**

Revelation 14:12,13

Here is the patience of the saints: here are they that keep the commandments of God, and the faith of Jesus. And I heard a voice from heaven saying unto me, Write, Blessed are the dead which die in the Lord from henceforth: Yea, saith the Spirit, that they may rest from their labours; and their works do follow them.

8. **SECOND SCRIPTURE READING:**

Revelation 21:3-7

And I heard a great voice out of heaven saying, Behold, the tabernacle of God is with men, and he will dwell with them, and they shall be his people, and God himself shall be with them, and be their God.

And God shall wipe away all tears from their eyes; and there shall be no more death, neither sorrow, nor crying, neither shall there be any more pain: for the former things are passed away. And he that sat upon the throne said,

Behold, I make all things new. And he said unto me, Write: for these words are true and faithful.

And he said unto me, It is done. I am Alpha and Omega, the beginning and the end. I will give unto him that is athirst of the fountain of the water of life freely. He that overcometh shall inherit all things; and I will be his God, and he shall be my son.

9. SONG: When I Survey the Wondrous Cross

When I survey the wondrous Cross
On which the Prince of Glory died
My richest gain I count but loss
And pour contempt on all my pride

Forbid it Lord that I should boast
Save in the death of Christ my God
All the vain things that charm me most
I sacrifice them to His blood

By Isaac Watts

10. BIOGRAPHY

11. TRIBUTES

12. SPECIAL SONG

13. OFFERTORY FOR FAMILY

14. SPECIAL SONG

15. SERMON

16. ALTAR CALL

17. CLOSING PRAYER

18. SONG: Now Thank We All Our God

Now thank we all our God
With hearts and hands and voices
Who wondrous things hath done
In whom this world rejoices
Who from our mothers' arms
Hath blessed us on our way
With countless gifts of love
And still is ours today.

All praise and thanks to God
The Father now be given
The Son and Him who reigns
With them in highest heaven
The one eternal God
Whom heaven and earth adore
For thus it was is now
And shall be evermore. Amen.

By Martin Rinckert

19. THE BENEDICTION

CHAPTER 13

Burial Service

And I heard a voice from heaven saying unto me, Write, Blessed are the dead which die in the Lord from henceforth: Yea, saith the Spirit, that they may rest from their labours; and their works do follow them.

Revelation 14:13

1. **PROCESSION TO THE CEMETERY** (Led by choir, then the coffin, officiating ministers, and all others in that order.)

2. **COFFIN PLACED ON SIDE OF THE GRAVE**

3. **OFFICIATING MINISTER TAKES HIS PLACE AT THE HEAD OF THE GRAVE**

4. **OPENING PRAYER**

5. **SONG: Lead Kindly Light**

Lead, kindly Light,
Amid the encircling gloom
Lead thou me on;
The night is dark,
and I am far from home,
Lead thou me on.
Keep thou my feet;
I do not ask to see
The distant scene; .
One step enough for me

I was not ever thus,
Nor prayed that Thou,
Shouldst lead me on;
I loved to choose,
And see my path but now
Lead thou me on.
I loved the garish,
Day and spite of fears
Pride ruled my will,
Remember not past years.

By John Henry Newman

6. **INSTRUCT THAT COFFIN BE LOWERED INTO THE GRAVE**

7. **SCRIPTURE READING**

1 Corinthians 15:51-58

Behold, I shew you a mystery; We shall not all sleep, but we shall all be changed, In a moment, in the twinkling of an eye, at the last trump: for the trumpet shall sound, and the dead shall be raised incorruptible, and we shall be changed. For this corruptible must put on incorruption, and this mortal must put on immortality. So when this corruptible shall have put on incorruption, and this mortal shall have put on immortality, then shall be brought to pass the saying that is written, Death is swallowed up in victory. O death, where is thy sting? O grave, where is thy victory?

The sting of death is sin; and the strength of sin is the law. But thanks be to God, which giveth us the victory through our Lord Jesus Christ. Therefore, my beloved brethren, be ye stedfast, unmoveable, always abounding in the work of the Lord, forasmuch as ye know that your labour is not in vain in the Lord.

8.   SONG: When Peace Like a River

When peace like a river attendeth my way,	**Chorus**
When sorrows like sea-billows roll;	*It is well (echo)*
Whatever my lot Thou has taught me to say,	*With my soul,(echo)*
"It is well, it is well,	*"It is well, it is well, with my*
with my soul."	*with my soul."*
	By Horacio Spafford

9.   PRAYER OF COMMITAL (To be read or alternatively, you may pray inspirationally as led by the Spirit of God.)

MINISTER: Let us pray

Heavenly Father, we come at this time to commit the body and the mortal remains of our brother/sister to the ground.

We take comfort in your scripture which says "for the Lord Himself will come down from heaven, with a loud command, with the voice of the archangel and with the trumpet call of God, and the dead in Christ will rise first."

After that, we who are still alive and are left will be caught up together with them in the clouds to meet the Lord in the air. And so we will be with the Lord for ever. We therefore encourage ourselves with these words.

As we commit this body into the ground we know that this is not a hopeless situation. We do it with HOPE and with faith in the name of Jesus Christ our Lord. Amen.

10.   COMMITAL (Minister takes shovel with soil in hand and says:)

- We look for the resurrection in the last day, and the appearing of the Lord Jesus, at whose second coming He shall judge the world.

- When the earth and sea shall give up the dead, and the dead in Christ shall rise first. Then we which are alive and remain shall be caught up together with them in the clouds.

- And then shall come to pass the saying that is written:

  Death is swallowed up in victory,
  O' death, where is thy sting
  O' grave, where is thy victory.

- For as much as the spirit of our deceased brother ...(Name of deceased)..., has returned to God who gave it, we therefore commit the body of ...(Name of deceased)... to the ground and to the dust.

- From earth to earth. (While sprinkling dust.)

- From dust to dust. (While sprinkling dust.)

- From ashes to ashes. (While sprinkling dust.)

- In the name of the Father, Son and Holy Ghost. Amen.

11.   PRAYER

12   SONG: Because He Lives

God sent His Son,
They called Him Jesus;
He came to love,
heal and forgive,
He lived and died
to buy my pardon,
An empty grave is there to prove ,
My Saviour lives!

Chorus:
Because He Lives I can face
tomorrow!
Because He lives all fear is
gone
And now I know He holds the
future
And life is worth the living,
just because He lives.
        By William J. Bill Gaither

13. **INVITATION OF FAMILY TO SPRINKLE DUST SYMBOLICALLY** (Invite three members of the family to sprinkle dust).

14. **PRESENTATION OF WREATHS** (Assisting Minister hands wreaths to Officiating Minister to read out the names.)

15. **VOTE OF THANKS** (To be given by a member of the family).

16. **CLOSING HYMN: Soon and very soon**

Soon and very soon
We are going to see the King
Soon and very soon
We are going to see the King
Hallelujah, Hallelujah
We are going to see the King

No more crying there
We are going to see the King
No more crying there
We are going to see the King
Hallelujah, Hallelujah
We are going to see the King

No more dying there...
No more sorrow there...
No more sadness there...
By Andraé Crouch

17. **CLOSING PRAYER**

18. **THE GRACE**

CHAPTER 14

Memorial & Thanksgiving Service

This is usually held after the Funeral and Burial services. It is a good occasion to let the bereaved family feel important and loved. As they are acknowledged publicly at the church service, a sense of brotherhood and belonging is established.

The family will never forget the attitude and commitment with which the ministers conducted themselves at the funeral of the relative. Allowing a member of the family to publicly address the church in a vote of thanks is a significant part of the ceremony which must not be omitted.

Praying for the family is also important. This ceremony can be interjected into a normal service without prolonging it unduly. It must be apt but brief.

1. INTRODUCTION

MINISTER: Dearly beloved, we would like at this time to perform the Memorial and Thanksgiving Service of our belated brother / sister / mother / father ...(Name of deceased)... whose sad event occurred at (Name of location) on ...(date of death)... The family is here with us today to thank God for His goodness and mercies and for seeing our brother through his lifetime.

Could the family please stand.

2. WORDS OF ENCOURAGEMENT TO THE FAMILY

MINISTER: Our (brother / sister / mother / father) is with the Lord which is a better place to be. We are confident, I say, and willing rather to be absent from the body, and to be present with the Lord.

The Holy Spirit Himself will comfort you since He is the Comforter. The Lord is the Father of the fatherless, the Husband of the widows and the Friend that sticketh closer than a brother.

3. PRAYER FOR THE FAMILY

MINISTER: Father, we thank you that your scripture is fulfiled today. This is the day that the Lord has made and we give thanks for it.

We pray for the family that you would comfort them and bless them.

We bring down every satanic projection and prediction against their lives, in Jesus' name.

We cancel, reverse and nullify every setback, limitation, disappointment, and frustration in their lives. We uproot every fear of the unknown and fear of death in their lives.

We cancel every assignment, claim and demand made against their very lives, in the name of Jesus.

We release them to serve the Lord with assurance that all things work together for good to them that love the Lord. Amen.

4. **VOTE OF THANKS AND ANNOUNCEMENTS** (A member of the family, who is pre-informed, is called up to give a vote of thanks and any relevant announcement.)

CHAPTER 15

Installation of Student Leaders

And the Lord said unto Moses, Gather unto me seventy men of the elders of Israel, whom thou knowest to be the elders of the people, and officers over them; and bring them unto the tabernacle of the congregation, that they may stand there with thee.

Numbers 11:16

1. **OPENING PRAYER**

2. **INCOMING AND OUTGOING STUDENT LEADERS TO COME TO THE FRONT**

3. **PRAYER FOR ALL STUDENT LEADERS**

4. **DECLARATION BY INCOMING STUDENT LEADERS** (Incoming leaders repeat after Officiating Minister).

- Thank you for the opportunity to work for God.

- Thank you for the trust you have bestowed on us.

- Thank you for the responsibility to do God's work.

- Pray for us that we will not fail you.

- Pray for us that we will not fail the Lord.

5. **DECLARATION TO OUTGOING STUDENT LEADERS** (By Officiating Minister)

- We are praying for you that you will not backslide as you leave the school.

- May you become a minister of the Gospel.

- May you be great in God's kingdom in Jesus' name.

6. **PRAYER**

7. **SYMBOLIC TRANSFER OF AUTHORITY THROUGH HANDSHAKE BETWEEN OUTGOING LEADERS AND INCOMING LEADERS**

8. **PLEDGE BY INCOMING STUDENT LEADERS**

1. According to John 10:11 which says "I am the good shepherd: the good shepherd giveth his life for the sheep." I WILL PRAY for my sheep and watch over their souls.

2. According to John 21:15 which says "So when they had dined, Jesus saith to Simon Peter, Simon, son of Jonas, lovest thou me more than these? He saith unto him, Yea, Lord; thou knowest that I love thee. He saith unto him, Feed my lambs." I PROMISE TO FEED my sheep with the Word in a way that they will understand and receive.

3. According to Jeremiah 23:2 which says "Therefore thus saith the LORD God of Israel against the pastors that feed my people; Ye have scattered my flock, and driven them away, and have not visited them: behold, I will visit upon you the evil of your doings, saith the LORD." I WILL VISIT my sheep lest the Lord visit my iniquities and my sins with His wrath.

4. According to John 21:16 which says" He saith to him again the second time, Simon, son of Jonas, lovest thou me? He saith unto him, Yea, Lord; thou knowest that I love thee. He saith unto him, Feed my sheep." I PROMISE TO TEND my sheep showing them the love and concern of the good shepherd.

5. According to 1Samuel 17:20 which says "And David rose up early in the morning, and left the sheep with a keeper, and took, and went, as Jesse had commanded him; and he came to the trench, as the host was going forth to the fight, and shouted for the battle." I WILL NOT LEAVE OR ABANDON my post and duty without providing a keeper for my sheep.

6. According to Revelation 3:19 which says "As many as I love, I rebuke and chasten: be zealous therefore, and repent." I WILL BE ZEALOUS.

7. According to John 17:12 which says "While I was with them in the world, I kept them in thy name: those that thou gavest me I have kept, and none of them is lost, but the son

of perdition; that the scripture might be fulfiled." I WILL NOT LOSE any of the sheep that the Lord has given to me.

8. According to 1 Thessalonians 5:12-13 which says "And we beseech you, brethren, to know them which labour among you, and are over you in the Lord, and admonish you; And to esteem them very highly in love for their work's sake. And be at peace among yourselves." I WILL HONOUR MY PASTORS AND TEACHERS who have taught me from the beginning.

I make these promises in the presence of Almighty God and before His servants solemnly freely and may God have mercy on my soul.

9. EXHORTATION

10. SONG: It's Our Time

To everything there is a season
To every purpose there is a time
The Lord who made the whole world
Has everything in his time
He wants the world to know Him
In all his righteousness
He has called us
into his kingdom
For such a time as this

Chorus
It's our time to believe
It's our time to love and live
There was a time we received
Now it's time for us to give
Standing hand in hand
together
Let's reach out and
touch our world
Can you hear the spirit
calling? It's our time

By Myles Munroe

11. SPECIAL SONG / OFFERING

12. COMMUNION

13. SONG: Take My Life and Let It Be

Take my life and let it be,
Consecrated Lord to thee,
Take my moments and my days,
Let them flow in ceaseless praise.

Take my hands, and let them move,
At the impulse of Thy love,
Take my feet, and let them be,
Swift and beautiful for Thee.

By Frances Ridley Havergal

14. CLOSING PRAYER

15. RECESSIONAL SONG: When We Walk With the Lord

When we walk with the Lord
In the light of His word
What a glory He sheds on our way!
While we do His good will
He abides with us still
And with all who will trust and obey

Chorus
Trust and obey
For there's no other way
To be happy in Jesus
Than to trust and obey

By John H. Sammis

CHAPTER 16

Appointment of Pastors

And I will give you pastors according to mine heart, which shall feed you with knowledge and understanding.

Jeremiah 3:15

1. **OPENING PRAYER**

2. **ASK PASTORAL APPOINTEES TO STAND**

3. **DECLARATION OF PURPOSE**

4. **SCRIPTURE READING**

John 15:15-16

Henceforth I call you not servants; for the servant knoweth not what his lord doeth: but I have called you friends; for all things that I have heard of my Father I have made known unto you.

Ye have not chosen me, but I have chosen you, and ordained you, that ye should go and bring forth fruit, and that your fruit should remain: that whatsoever ye shall ask of the Father in my name, he may give it you.

5. **SONG: When We Walk With the Lord**

When we walk with the Lord
In the light of His word
What a glory He sheds on our way!
While we do His good will
He abides with us still
And with all who will trust and obey

Chorus
Trust and obey
For there's no other way
To be happy in Jesus
Than to trust and obey
By John H. Sammis

6. **PASTORAL APPOINTEES TO STEP FORWARD**
(If they are too many ask them to come to the altar)

7. **OFFICIATING MINISTER PRAYS FOR THE CANDIDATES**

8. **A CHARGE TO THE CANDIDATES**

9. **PRESENTATION OF CROSSES AND CERTIFICATES TO THE CANDIDATES** (by the officiating minister & assisting ministers)

10. **OFFICIATING MINISTER LEADS CANDIDATES TO SAY THE PASTORS' PLEDGE**

PASTORS' PLEDGE

1. According to Jeremiah 3:15 which says: "And I will give you pastors according to mine heart, which shall feed you with knowledge and understanding." I WILL FEED my sheep with knowledge and understanding.

2. According to Hebrews 13:17 which says: "Obey them that have the rule over you, and submit yourselves: for they watch for your souls, as they that must give account, that they may do it with joy, and not with grief: for that is unprofitable for you." I WILL ACCOUNT FOR all my sheep to my pastors and to the Lord Jesus on the judgment day. May the Lord help me to do this with joy and not with grief.

3. According to 1 Corinthians 9:18 which says: "What is my reward then? Verily that, when I preach the gospel, I may make the gospel of Christ without charge, that I abuse not my power in the gospel." I SHALL MAKE THE GOSPEL WITHOUT CHARGE and not abuse my power in the gospel.

4. According to John 17:12 which says: "While I was with them in the world, I kept them in thy name: those that thou gavest me I have kept, and none of them is lost, but the son of perdition; that the scripture might be fulfiled." I WILL ENDEAVOUR TO BE HUMBLE AND CHILDLIKE throughout my life and ministry.

5. According to 2 Corinthians 4:1 which says: "Therefore seeing we have this ministry, as we have received mercy, we faint not;" I WILL NOT FAINT nor be weary of the ministry because I have received mercy.

6. According to 2 Timothy 4:5 which says: "But watch thou in all things, endure afflictions, do the work of an evangelist, make full proof of thy ministry." I WILL FULFIL my ministry.

7. According to 2 Timothy 4:8 which says: "Henceforth there is laid up for me a crown of righteousness, which the Lord, the righteous judge, shall give me at that day: and not to me only, but unto all them also that love his appearing." I PROMISE TO BE WATCHFUL to endure all things and to lay hold, one day, on the crown of righteousness.

8. According to Titus 2:11 which says: "For the grace of God that bringeth salvation hath appeared to all men," I SHALL ENDEAVOUR TO SHARE the grace that bringeth salvation until the last man has heard.

I make these promises in the presence of Almighty God and before His servants solemnly, freely and may God have mercy on my soul.

11. INTRODUCTION OF NEW PASTORS TO THE CONGREGATION

12. CLOSING PRAYER

13. RECESSION

CHAPTER 17

Ordination of Pastors

And I will give you pastors according to mine heart, which shall feed you with knowledge and understanding.

Jeremiah 3:15

ORDINATION OF PASTORS

1. **PROCESSION** (Candidates file in from the back followed by officiating ministers. Congregation asked to stand)

2. **PROCESSIONAL HYMN: Stand Up, Stand Up For Jesus**

Stand up, stand up for Jesus
Ye soldiers of the cross
Lift high His royal banner;
It must not suffer loss
From victory unto victory,
His army shall He lead
Till every foe is vanquished,
And Christ is Lord indeed

Stand up, stand up for Jesus
The trumpet-call obey
Forth to the mighty conflict;
In this His glorious day!
Ye that are men, now serve Him;
Against unnumbered foes
Let courage rise with danger,
And strength to strength oppose

By George Duffield Jr.

3. **OPENING PRAYER**

4. **DECLARATION OF PURPOSE (Congregation sits)**

MINISTER: What is our purpose? Our purpose for assembling in today in the presence of God is to ordain these ministers to the ministry of our Lord Jesus Christ, bearing in mind the words of our Lord when He sent forth His disciples and gave them power against unclean spirits, to cast them out, and to heal all manner of sickness and all manner of disease.

Jesus said, "As ye go, preach saying, "The kingdom of heaven is at hand. Heal the sick, cleanse the lepers, raise the dead, cast out devils: freely ye have received, freely give".

As we ordain these persons, we acknowledge that their real ordination comes from above. Because Jesus said, "Ye have not chosen me but I have chosen you and ordained you that you should go forth and bring forth fruit and that your fruit should remain, that whatsoever you may ask the Father in my name, He may give it you."

■ Who can therefore be ordained? We must ordain into the ministry a kind of man who looks at things from a heavenly viewpoint and not an earthly one.

A man that has an understanding of God's nature and purpose through His word, and trembles at that Word so that he will not disobey even the smallest commandment or neglect to teach it to others.

A man who lives, not by the promptings of their own reason, but by the leading of the Holy Spirit.

A man who has a longing to see others not only saved, but also made disciples of Christ, and brought to the knowledge of the truth and to obedience to all of God's commandments,

A man of living faith who has no confidence in himself or natural abilities but complete confidence in God as the unfailing helper in all situations. What is ordination? Ordination is the culmination of a long and exacting process in which the individual has responded to the call of God on his life and has been observed, trained, assessed and accepted by those senior to him in the ministry, and has demonstrated to the congregation as one indeed called of God, and as one ready to take up the responsibility of the preaching of Christ.

Ordination is the process by which propriety is introduced into the church and by which Eldership and Leadership are clearly defined and set apart for the purposes of order, ranking and structure.

Ordination confers on the individual all the rights and privileges of the ordained Minister, including the authority to solemnize marriages, conduct burials and baptisms, and conduct all forms of religious worship and sacramental functions, in accordance with the tenets of this church, so long as he maintains godly, moral and biblical standards.

Into which privileged estate these persons present come now to be installed. The profiles of the candidates shall now be presented to the congregation.

5.   **READING OF PROFILES** (Candidates stand and face congregation during the reading of their profile by the Assisting Minister. Where there are numerous candidates, profiles will not be read but congregation shall be asked to refer to the programmes).

6.   **ORDINATION VOWS** (Ask candidates to stand)

MINISTER: I require and charge you as you will answer on the Day of Judgment when the secrets of all hearts will be disclosed that if you know of any impediment why you may not be ordained into the ministry of the Lord Jesus Christ, you do now confess it.

MINISTER: (Candidates repeating after) I solemnly declare that I know not of any lawful impediment why I, (Name of Candidate), may not be ordained into the ministry of the Lord Jesus Christ. I therefore declare that as far as my conscience serves me, I am blameless, the husband of one wife, sober, of good behaviour, given to hospitality and apt to teach.

I am not given to wine, not greedy of filthy lucre, not covetous, not a novice, not violent, but rule well my own house and have a good reputation with those outside the church.

MINISTER: Do you take this ministry of the Lord Jesus Christ freely and willingly and do you promise to live and to preach the Gospel so long as you will be alive upon this earth

CANDIDATES: I do

MINISTER: Do you seriously consider the responsibility, the weight of the work involved and the sacrifices you and your family may be called upon to make in your lifetime.

CANDIDATES: I do

MINISTER: Do you look on the fields that are white unto harvest; do you take upon yourself the care of the church; do you pledge to keep before your heart that call that set you apart?

CANDIDATES: I do

MINISTER: (Candidates repeating after) I, ...(Name of Candidate)..., hereby declare that being motivated and constrained by the love of God, and not by the desire for position or earthly gain, leave the ranks of ordinary Christian laity and enter into the ranks of the high calling of God to the ministry of the Lord Jesus Christ.

7. **ORDINATION PRAYER** (Laying on of hands / anointing with oil; candidates may kneel or lie down)

8. **SONG : A Charge to Keep I Have**

A charge to keep I have,
A God to glorify
A never-dying should to save,
And fit it for the sky

O serve the present age,
My calling to fulfil
O may it all my powers engage,
To do my Master's will

By Charles Wesley

9. OFFERING AND SPECIAL SONG

10. FIRST SCRIPTURE READING:

Colossians 3:1-4

If ye then be risen with Christ, seek those things which are above, where Christ sitteth on the right hand of God. Set your affection on things above, not on things on the earth. For ye are dead, and your life is hid with Christ in God. When Christ, who is our life, shall appear, then shall ye also appear with him in glory.

11. SECOND SCRIPTURE READING:

Colossians 4:1-4

Masters, give unto your servants that which is just and equal; knowing that ye also have a Master in heaven. Continue in prayer, and watch in the same with thanksgiving; Withal praying also for us, that God would open unto us a door of utterance, to speak the mystery of Christ, for which I am also in bonds: That I may make it manifest, as I ought to speak.

12. SPECIAL SONG BY PSALMIST

13. SERMON

14. MINISTER'S PLEDGE (Candidates stand and face congregation whilst reading)

1. According to 1 Corinthians 9:16, which says "For though I preach the gospel, I have nothing to glory of: for necessity is laid upon me; yea, woe is unto me, if I preach not the gospel!" I PLEDGE MYSELF TO THE SERVICE of God and to the Ministry of the Lord Jesus Christ.

2. According to 1 Corinthians 1:10, which says "Now I beseech you, brethren, by the name of our Lord Jesus Christ, that ye all speak the same thing, and that there be no divisions

among you; but that ye be perfectly joined together in the same mind and in the same judgment" I PLEDGE TO ALIGN MYSELF to the vision, principles and spirit of the ministry wherever God shall place me.

3. According to 2 Timothy 4:7, which says "I have fought a good fight, I have finished my course, I have kept the faith": I WILL FIGHT A GOOD FIGHT

4. According to 1 Corinthians 4:2, which says "Moreover it is required in stewards, that a man be found faithful." I PLEDGE TO BE LOYAL AND FAITHFUL in my conduct, speech and attitude.

5. According to 1 Peter 5:2, which says "Feed the flock of God which is among you, taking the oversight thereof, not by constraint, but willingly; not for filthy lucre, but of a ready mind" I SHALL NOT BE MOTIVATED BY FINANCIAL GAIN nor dishonourably motivated by the advantages and profits belonging to my office.

6. According to 1 Corinthians 4:15, which says "For though ye have ten thousand instructors in Christ, yet have ye not many fathers: for in Christ Jesus I have begotten you through the gospel." I PLEDGE TO RESPECT AND HONOUR the seniors, the fathers and the patriarchs of ministry.

7. According to Colossians 3:2-3, which says "Set your affection on things above, not on things on the earth. For ye are dead, and your life is hid with Christ in God." I PLEDGE TO ALWAYS BE MINDED of eternity and eternal judgments.

8. According to Luke 17:10 which says "So likewise ye, when ye shall have done all those things which are commanded you, say, We are unprofitable servants: we have done that which was our duty to do" and 1 Peter 5:3, which says "Neither as being lords over God's heritage, but being ensamples to the flock." MY ROLE IN THE CHURCH shall be that of a humble servant and not a Lord.

9. According to 2 Timothy 4:7 which says "I have fought a good fight, I have finished my course, I have kept the faith" I PLEDGE TO KEEP THE FAITH, finish my course and fulfil my ministry and may God have mercy on me in the day of judgment.

I make these promises in the presence of Almighty God and before His servants solemnly, freely and may God have mercy on my soul.

fulfil my ministry and may God have mercy on me in the day of judgment.

I make these promises in the presence of Almighty God and before His servants solemnly, freely and may God have mercy on my soul.

15. **SPECIAL SONG BY PSALMIST**

16. **PRESENTATION TO INDIVIDUALS** (Certificates, cross, prayer, laying on of hands, anointing with oil)

17. **FINAL PRAYER FOR ALL CANDIDATES**

18. **RECESSION** (Newly-ordained pastors file out file out ahead of officiating ministers)

19. **SONG: Take My Life and Let It Be**

Take my life and let it be,   *Take my hands, and let them move.*
Consecrated Lord to thee   *At the impulse of Thy love*
Take my moments and my days;   *Take my feet, and let them be;*
Let them flow in ceaseless praise   *Swift and beautiful for Thee*

20. **OFFICIAL PICTURES TAKEN**

- Officiating Ministers and Ordained Pastors

- Individual pictures – Ordained Pastors with spouses

CHAPTER 18

Consecration of a Bishop / Apostle / Prophet

This is a true saying, If a man desire the office of a bishop, he desireth a good work.

1 Timothy 3:1

1. **OPENING PRAYER / INTRODUCTION OF PROCESSION**

2. **SONG: How Great Thou Art**

> *O Lord my God, When I in awesome wonder*
> *Consider all the worlds thy hand has made*
> *I see the stars, I hear the roaring thunder*
> *Thy power throughout the universe displayed*

> *Then sings my soul,*
> *My Saviour God to thee*
> *How great thou art*
> *How great thou art*
> *Written by Carl Boberg*
> *(Translated by Stuart K Hine)*

(Order of Procession)

a. Assisting Ceremonial Ministers bearing vestments, staff and Bibles

b. Candidate (in white cassock)

c. Fully-robed Guest Bishops/Assisting Bishops

d. Bearer of the Consecrating Bishop's Sword

e. Bearer of the Consecrating Bishop's Bible

f. Bearer of the Consecrating Bishop's Staff

g. Consecrating Bishop wearing Mitre on skull cap for procession

3. **REMOVAL OF MITRE**

4. **PRAYER BY CONSECRATING BISHOP** (Candidates kneel before the altar whilst congregation stands)

5. **PURPOSE OF SERVICE** (Ask candidates to stand and congregation to sit)

CONSECRATING BISHOP:

■ What is consecration? Consecration is the act of installing men with spiritual authority and spiritual dignity who will stand alone for God in the world, if need be. Totally uncompromising men like the apostles and prophets of old.

- Consecration is the act of installing men who know how to pray without ceasing and also how to fast and pray when needed. These Apostles, Prophets and Bishops are willing to be all things to all men so that by all means they will save some.

- Consecration is the act of installing men full of mercy who can sympathise with the worst of sinners and the worst of believers and have hope for them because they consider themselves to be the chiefest amongst sinners. They shall have a special care for the poor, the sick, the naked, the hungry and the prisoners.

- Consecration is therefore the act of installing Apostles, Prophets and Bishops as men who will proclaim the whole counsel of God to feed the sheep. Bishops will expose religious harlotry and unscriptural human traditions because they have the revelation of the Holy Spirit.

- Consecration is the act of installing Apostles, Prophets and Bishops who desire to please no human being on the face of the earth but have a burning passion to see Christ glorified in the church.

- Consecration is the act of installing men who are to preside over the ordination of pastors and reverend ministers, and to join together in the consecration of others.

- What kind of men can be consecrated? We must consecrate into the ministry the kind of men worthy of the high calling of God. They must be men of several distinctions and qualities.

- They must be men that will stand before His face and hear His voice daily.

- They must be men who have no desire in their hearts for anyone or anything other than God Himself.

- They must be men who are so rooted and grounded in humility that neither human praise nor spiritual growth, neither a divinely endorsed ministry nor anything else will be able to make them lose the awareness of their being less than all the saints.

- Bishops must be men who have been disciplined successfully by God in the fires of affliction, abuse, tribulations, false accusations, physical sickness, financial hardships and opposition from relatives and religious leaders.

- Bishops must be men who will never be influenced by their wives, children, relatives, friends or other believers to cool off in their obedience to Christ to God's commandments.

- Bishops must be men who will make no distinction between the millionaire and the beggar, the white-skinned and the dark-skinned, the intellectual and the idiot, the cultured and the barbarian, but who will treat them all alike.

- They must be men who have forsaken all and who are not attracted anymore to money or material things and who desire no gifts from others. Such men can trust God for all their earthly needs and never hint about their material needs.

- They must be men who cannot be pressurized by others in their labours in the Lord, either in conversation or through letters and reports.

- God's work in the world suffers today because there are few men who have a longing and a burning passion to see Christ glorified in the church.

- Bishops therefore must be men who will walk in His will and do His work on the earth. From amongst us He calls and draws men to be fully dedicated to His service and to His house, men who need no earthly honours or titles to be offered them for their labours in God.

- Bishops must be men who will minister to the needs of the multitudes who seek Him. He has raised up men who are anointed of the Holy Spirit to feed His flock.

- Bishops are men who live constantly under the anointing of the Holy Spirit, endowed with the supernatural gifts He has given them. These men know that the church is the body of Christ and give all their energies, their material wealth and spiritual gifts to build the church.

- What therefore is our purpose today?

- Our purpose for gathering is to consecrate such men to the high office of a Bishop.

6. PRAYER

7. READING OF PROFILES (Each candidate stands as his profile is read, all other candidates to be seated).

8. SONG: Take My Life and Let It Be

Take my life and let it be,   *Take my hands, and let them move.*
Consecrated Lord to thee   *At the impulse of Thy love*
Take my moments and my days;   *Take my feet, and let them be;*
Let them flow in ceaseless praise   *Swift and beautiful for Thee*

By Frances Ridley Havergal

9. FIRST SCRIPTURE READING

Hebrews 5:1-10

For every high priest taken from among men is ordained for men in things pertaining to God, that he may offer both gifts and sacrifices for sins: Who can have compassion on the ignorant, and on them that are out of the way; for that he himself also is compassed with infirmity. And by reason hereof he ought, as for the people, so also for himself, to offer for sins.

93

And no man taketh this honour unto himself, but he that is called of God, as was Aaron. So also Christ glorified not himself to be made an high priest; but he that said unto him, Thou art my Son, today have I begotten thee.

As he saith also in another place, Thou art a priest for ever after the order of Melchisedec. Who in the days of his flesh, when he had offered up prayers and supplications with strong crying and tears unto him that was able to save him from death, and was heard in that he feared; Though he were a Son, yet learned he obedience by the things which he suffered; And being made perfect, he became the author of eternal salvation unto all them that obey him; Called of God an high priest after the order of Melchisedec.

10. SPECIAL SONG BY PSALMIST

11. SECOND SCRIPTURE READING

Isaiah 42:1-9

Behold my servant, whom I uphold; mine elect, in whom my soul delighteth; I have put my spirit upon him: he shall bring forth judgment to the Gentiles. He shall not cry, nor lift up, nor cause his voice to be heard in the street. A bruised reed shall he not break, and the smoking flax shall he not quench: he shall bring forth judgment unto truth. He shall not fail nor be discouraged, till he have set judgment in the earth: and the isles shall wait for his law.

Thus saith God the LORD, he that created the heavens, and stretched them out; he that spread forth the earth, and that which cometh out of it; he that giveth breath unto the people upon it, and spirit to them that walk therein: I the LORD have called thee in righteousness, and will hold thine hand, and will keep thee, and give thee for a covenant of the people, for a light of the Gentiles; To open the blind eyes, to bring out the prisoners from the prison, and them that sit in darkness out of the prison house.

I am the LORD: that is my name: and my glory will I not give to another, neither my praise to graven images. Behold, the former things are come to pass, and new things do I declare: before they spring forth I tell you of them.

12. **SPECIAL SONG BY PSALMIST**

13. **CONSECRATION VOWS** (Ask all candidates to stand)

CONSECRATING BISHOP: Will you obey the call of God and fulfil the ministry and office of a Bishop / Apostle / Prophet in His church?

CANDIDATE: I will

CONSECRATING BISHOP: Will you preserve the doctrine of the Christian faith, of salvation, of the blood of Jesus and of the cross of Jesus Christ?

CANDIDATE: I will

CONSECRATING BISHOP: Will you adhere to the accountability of your conscience and the Holy Scriptures?

CANDIDATE: I will

CONSECRATING BISHOP: Will you be diligent in prayer, in reading the Holy Scriptures, and in all studies that will deepen your faith and understanding of the mysteries of God?

CANDIDATE: I will

14. **PRAYER**

15. **ASK CONGREGATION TO STAND AND ADDRESS THEM.**

CONSECRATING BISHOP: Brothers and sisters, you have heard how great is the charge that these candidates are ready to undertake, and you have heard their declarations. Is it now your will that they should be consecrated? Say "It is" if you agree.

CONGREGATION: It is

CONSECRATING BISHOP: Will you continually pray for them? Say "We will" if you agree to do so.

CONGREGATION: We will

CONSECRATING BISHOP: Will you uphold and encourage them in their ministry? Say 'We will' if you will.

CONGREGATION: We will

CONSECRATING BISHOP: Will you rebel against them and oppose them in their duties? Say 'We will not' if you will not rebel.

CONGREGATION: We will not

CONSECRATING BISHOP: Will you undermine their authority and betray them in the course of their ministry? Say 'We will not' if you will not undermine and betray them.

CONGREGATION: We will not

CONSECRATING BISHOP: Will you challenge their authority on a daily basis and make things difficult for them? Say 'We will not' if you will not challenge their authority.

CONGREGATION: We will not

16. **PRAYERS AND ANOINTING OF CANDIDATES WITH HORN OF OIL** (Candidates kneel before Consecrating Bishop and the congregation stands)

17. **COMMUNION FOR NEW BISHOPS / APOSTLES / PROPHETS**

*** FROM THIS POINT IN THE CEREMONY, THE PRESENTATION IS DONE FOR EACH CANDIDATE SEPARATELY. ***

18. **PRESENTATION OF THE VESTMENTS** (ASK EACH CANDIDATE TO COME FORWARD TO RECEIVE VESTMENTS.)

CONSECRATING BISHOP:

- When the Lord commanded Moses to consecrate Aaron that he might minister in the high priest's office, he was bidden to take with him sacrifices and the garments which had been prepared. He was to bring Aaron before the Lord in the presence of the entire congregation, to wash him with water, to put upon him the holy garments, to anoint him with holy oil, and to offer sacrifices for the atonement of his sins. These things instruct us that there is a holy order appointed in the church. They are set forth as types and shadows in the church.

- In fulfilment of this order, our brother has been washed and cleansed with the Word. He is now to be robed in the holy garments of the priesthood. He has been anointed with oil and with the Holy Spirit.

- The Candidate entered in a white tunic, a belt and cross.

- The white tunic is a symbol of that holiness and purity which the Lord commanded, "Let thy priests be clothed with righteousness." White is also a visual reminder that "He that overcometh, the same shall be clothed in white raiment."

- The belt denotes the priest's readiness to serve the Lord and is also a sign that he is bound to Christ.

■ The cross is worn as a reminder of the sacrifice required to follow Jesus.

19. **PRESENTATION OF THE COPE** (Assisting Minister fetches the Cope when Consecrating Bishop declares):

■ The Cope symbolizes the shepherd's covering of the sheep from their vulnerability and exposure. As you wear this cope, may the Lord cover you from the arrows of the enemy and may you in the same way cover the flock over which the Holy Ghost has made you overseer.

(Consecrating Bishop robes the Bishop / Apostle / Prophet with the assistance of Assisting Ceremonial Ministers)

20. **PRESENTATION OF THE MITRE** (Assisting Minister fetches the Mitre when Consecrating Bishop declares):

■ The Mitre derived from the Greek word 'mitra' signifies a head dress or a headband.

■ The head dress symbolizes both the crown of thorns and the authority entrusted to Bishops as leaders of the Church.

■ The pointed ends of the Mitre symbolize the cloven tongues on the heads of the disciples on the day of Pentecost.

■ The streamers represent the everlasting living water that Christ offers to the believer.

■ Wear this Mitre with the understanding that your Master wore a crown of thorns on the cross, and if you are faithful to the end, you will receive a crown of glory when the Lord appears.

(Consecrating Bishop places Mitre on Bishop / Apostle / Prophet with assistance of Assisting Ceremonial Ministers)

21. **PRESENTATION OF THE RING (Assisting Minister fetches the Ring when Consecrating Bishop declares):**

- The Ring is a symbol of sonship and honour. Our Lord depicts the father as giving a ring to the son in the Parable of the Prodigal Son. The Ring symbolizes the restoration and establishment of the returning son to his position of honoured sonship.

- The Ring is worn on the right hand (the hand that represents God given authority), just as Christ sits on the right hand of God the Father. Receive this Ring as the token of the link which binds you to our Lord, and as a symbol of your sonship and office

(Consecrating Bishop places the Ring on finger of Candidate with assistance of Assisting Ceremonial Ministers)

22. **PRESENTATION OF THE BIBLE** (Assisting Minister fetches the Bible when Consecrating Bishop declares):

- Take these Holy Scriptures. They shall be the light of your life and ministry. These scriptures shall give you access to God and to God's mind and will. Through these scriptures, you shall fellowship with other great prophets and servants of the Lord. Only within these pages shall you find other like-minded servants whose hearts are fixed on heaven, on God and on eternity.

(Consecrating Bishop gives Bible to the candidate with assistance of Assisting Ceremonial Ministers)

23. **PRESENTATION OF THE STAFF (Assisting Minister fetches the Staff when Consecrating Bishop declares):**

   ■ The Staff is the traditional symbol of a shepherd. This Staff is presented because the Bishop is first and foremost a shepherd. Like the rod of Moses, it is the symbol of your authority and the symbol of God's power and presence with you.

   (Consecrating Bishop presents Staff to Candidate with assistance of Assisting Ceremonial Ministers)

24. **PRESENTATION OF CERTIFICATE AND LICENSE** (Consecrating Bishop reads and presents certificate)

   *** *AT THIS POINT, RESTART*
   PRESENTATION OF VESTMENTS
   FOR THE NEXT CANDIDATE. ***
   (GO BACK TO POINT 18)

25. **SPECIAL SONG**

26. **PRESENTATION OF NEW BISHOPS / APOSTLES / PROPHETS TO THE CONGREGATION** (Ask new Bishops / Apostles / Prophets to turn round and face congregation for salutation and a wave).

27. **SPECIAL SONG BY PSALMIST**

28. **FIRST OFFERING**

29. **SERMON**

30. **SPEECHES BY GUEST / ROBED BISHOPS**

31. **MAIDEN SPEECHES BY THE NEW BISHOPS / APOSTLES / PROPHETS**

32. **SECOND OFFERING**

33. **SPECIAL SONG** (with new Bishops / Apostles / Prophets facing congregation while congregation keeps standing)

34. **CLOSING PRAYER**

35. **RECESSIONAL TEAM LINE UP FOR RECESSION**

36. **ORDER OF RECESSION**

   a. New Bishops / Apostles / Prophets (each holding his own staff)

   b. Assisting Ceremonial Ministers bearing Bibles and Certificates of New Bishops

   c. Guest / fully-robed Bishops

   d. Bearer of the Consecrating Bishop's Sword

   e. Bearer of the Consecrating Bishop's Bible

   f. Bearer of the Consecrating Bishop's Staff

   g. Consecrating Bishop

   h. Clergy

37. **WEARING OF THE MITRE FOR RECESSION**

38. **RECESSIONAL SONG: To God be the Glory**

Chorus:

To God be the glory,
Great things He hath done
So loved He the world that
He gave us His Son
Who yielded His life
An atonement for sin
And opened the life gate
that all may go in

Praise the Lord! Praise the Lord!
Let the earth hear His voice
Praise the Lord! Praise the Lord,
Let the people rejoice
O come to the Father
  through Jesus the Son
And give Him the glory great things
  He hath done

By Fanny Crossby

39. **GREETINGS AND PHOTOGRAPHS**